A Practical Guide to
Good Bookkeeping and
Business Systems

A PRACTICAL GUIDE TO GOOD BOOKKEEPING AND BUSINESS SYSTEMS

John Kellock

BUSINESS BOOKS

London Melbourne Sydney Auckland Johannesburg

Business Books Ltd

An imprint of the Hutchinson Publishing Group

17–21 Conway Street, London W1P 6JD

Hutchinson Group (Australia) Pty Ltd
30–32 Cremorne Street, Richmond South, Victoria 3121
PO Box 151, Broadway, New South Wales 2007

Hutchinson Group (NZ) Ltd
32–34 View Road, PO Box 40–086, Glenfield, Auckland 10

Hutchinson Group (SA) (Pty) Ltd
PO Box 337, Bergvlei 2012, South Africa

First published 1982
Reprinted 1982

Set in Times

Printed in Great Britain by The Anchor Press Ltd
and bound by Wm Brendon & Son Ltd,
both of Tiptree, Essex

British Library Cataloguing in Publication Data
Kellock, John
  A practical guide to good bookkeeping and
  business systems.
  1. Office practice.
  I. Title
  651'.028   HF5547.5

ISBN 0 09 147410 8

Contents

To the Businessman

Purpose   The purpose of this book is to provide the businessman with:

□ An understanding of a bookkeeping system from recording of business transactions to preparation of final accounts in the form of trading and profit and loss accounts and balance sheet.

□ The techniques used for analysing and interpreting the financial statements used in a business.

□ A brief description of a microcomputer system of bookkeeping and the points to consider when purchasing this type of equipment.

□ An introduction to the Kalamazoo Bookkeeping System for Small Businesses with full instructions on how to install and operate the system.

How to use the book   The book is intended to be used by the businessman as a reference manual to enable him:

□ To instal and operate a bookkeeping system for recording business transactions.

□ To analyse and interpret final accounts and to use the information obtained for controlling the business.

□ To assist in staff training in bookkeeping and accounting procedures.

□ To achieve these objectives, the book covers the following main problems:

Understanding business accounting
How to set up your bookkeeping system
How to prepare your final accounts
How to analyse and interpret your final accounts
How to instal and operate the Kalamazoo Bookkeeping System for Small Businesses

Main features   □ The book is written as a complete guide to bookkeeping for the businessman who is about to start up or who is presently running a small business.

□ The sections are written in easy-to-follow style with simple instructions on how to enter business transactions in the bookkeeping records with suitable examples included to illustrate each topic.

□ The layout allows the businessman to use the book as a complete manual for the bookkeeping system of the business or as a reference book for information on bookkeeping and accounting methods.

□ A useful section relating to the use of the microcomputer in a small business is included.

□ Included in the book are comprehensive instructions on how to instal and operate the Kalamazoo Bookkeeping System for Small Businesses.

7

Part 1 Understanding Business Accounting

9

1 Controlling Your Business

What is accounting?

Accounting provides information about business enterprises to interested parties. This information may relate to past performance, present position or future prospects. Financial accounting consists of recording, classifying, presenting and interpreting business transactions.

How can accounting help the businessman

A good accounting system can provide the businessman with information without which it would be difficult, if not impossible, to conduct his business activities. The main information provided by an accounting system would include:

- Income from retail sales, or invoiced work in the case of a tradesman or manufacturer, for the period.
- The total costs of operating the business.
- The profit or loss for the period.
- The amount of money due to the business from customers.
- The amount of money owed by the business to suppliers.
- The amount of cash in the bank and on hand.
- The total value of the business' assets.
- The total liabilities of the business.
- The amount of capital invested in the business.

The main types of business enterprise

Sole Proprietor or Trader In this type of business the ownership is vested in one person although there may be employees.

Partnership This form of business is carried on by two or more owners who have invested capital in the business with a view to making a profit.

Limited Compa::y This type of business is a separate legal entity subject to the Companies Acts. The owners of the business are referred to as shareholders and are allotted shares in return for their investment in the company.

Features to look for in a business accounting system

- It must be capable of recording the basic business transactions entered into by the business, e.g. sales, purchases and wages.
- It must be simple to operate.
- It must be cheap to use and easily understood by clerical staff.
- It must satisfy Customs and Excise for VAT purposes.
- It must enable transactions to be recorded such that final accounts in the form of trading and profit and loss accounts and balance sheet can be extracted by the businessman or his accountant.
- For a limited company, it must satisfy the requirements of the Companies Acts in respect of the records to be kept.

2 How to Record Business Transactions

What is a business transaction?

A business transaction is any exchange or transfer of goods or services in monetary terms.

Types of business transaction

Let us assume A. Smith commences business on 1 January with £1,000 in the bank. On 3 January he purchases goods for £500 and pays for them in cash. On 10 January he sells half the goods for cash and receives £400 for them. What information can be gained from these transactions?

Question	Answer		
			£
What is the capital at the start of the business?	The amount paid in by A. Smith:		1,000
What purchases were made during the period?	The total amount of goods bought:		500
What sales were made during the period?	The total amount of goods sold:		400
What profit was made in the period?	The profit is calculated thus:		
	Sales for period		400
	Less: Purchases	500	
	Less: stock in hand	250	250
	Profit for period		150
How much money was in the bank at the the end of the period?	Balance at start		1,000
	Add: Received from sales		400
			1,400
	Less: paid out for purchases		500
	Balance at end of period		900
What stock was in the business at the end of the period?	Goods bought		500
	Less: Cost of goods sold		250
	Stock in hand		250
What assets were in the business at the end of the period?	The assets in the business are:		
	Balance in bank		900
	Stock in hand		250
	Total assets		1,150
What was the capital in the business at the end of the period?	Capital at start		1,000
	Add: Profit for period		150
	Capital at end		1,150

How to classify business transactions

Transactions can be classified as:

1 *Cash transactions* — where goods or services and cash change hands at the same time.
2 *Credit transactions* — where goods or services are supplied but payment by the buyer is made at a later date.

12

Classification of accounts

Type	Description	Examples	
Assets	Items that are owned by the business	Land Buildings Motor vehicles Plant and machinery Goodwill Fixtures and fittings	Stock Debtors Loan to persons or company Cash at bank Cash in hand
Liabilities	Amounts owed by the business to outside parties	Bank overdraft Creditors	Loan from a person or company
Capital	The owner's investment in the business – the excess of assets over liabilities	Capital account of owner Partners' capital accounts Share capital	— Sole trader — Partnership — Limited company
Expenses	Amounts incurred by the business for the purchase of goods and services used within a short period	Purchase of goods for resale Salaries and wages Advertising Bad debts Bank interest Carriage Commission Customs duty Depreciation Discount allowed Electricity Insurance	Motor expenses Office expenses Packing Power Rates Rent Repairs Stationery Sundry expenses Telephone Travelling Selling expenses
Income	Amounts received by the business from sales and other services	Sales of goods Interest received	Commission received Discount received

How to record business transactions in a ledger

A ledger is a book in which a summary of all business transactions is recorded in *ledger accounts*.

- ☐ Each ledger consists of a series of accounts.
- ☐ Each account has two sides – a debit side and a credit side.
- ☐ Details of each business transaction are recorded in the appropriate ledger account.
- ☐ An account may refer to a person or company, or be in respect of an asset, liability, capital, expense or income.
- ☐ Each ledger account has a folio number included for reference purposes.

13

Structure of a ledger account

DR.			W. Brown a/c			(B1)	CR.
Date	Details	Folio	Amount	Date	Details	Folio	Amount
			£				£
Jan 5	Goods	SDB/1	50.00	Jan 10	Bank	CB/1	50.00
①	②	③	④	⑤	⑥	⑦	⑧

Key to ledger accounts
Columns 1 and 5 Date of transaction
Columns 2 and 6 Description of transaction
Columns 3 and 7 Reference to the accounting book which records the other aspect of the transaction
Columns 4 and 8 Amount of transaction
Columns 1–4 record the entries on the debit side of the account
Columns 5–8 record the entries on the credit side of the account
Note The folio of the above ledger account is B1.

Alternative structure of above ledger account

		W. Brown a/c			
Date	Details	Folio	DR.	CR.	Balance
			£	£	£
Jan 5	Goods	SDB/1	50.00		50.00
10	Bank	CB/1		50.00	—

What is double-entry bookkeeping?

The principle of double-entry bookkeeping states that every business transaction has two aspects:

DEBIT   and   CREDIT

How to record instructions in a double-entry system

Classification of accounts	Entry to record an increase	Entry to record a decrease
Asset	Debit	Credit
Liability	Credit	Debit
Capital	Credit	Debit
Expenses	Debit	Credit
Income	Credit	Debit

How to analyse a transaction and record it in the business books

☐ Establish which two accounts are affected by the transaction.
☐ Classify the accounts affected by the transaction under the following categories: asset, liability, capital, expense or income.
☐ Determine if the accounts are increased or decreased by the transaction.
☐ Record the entries in the accounts according to the instructions given above.

Illustration

Recording a transaction in the ledger using the double-entry system of bookkeeping

A. Smith purchased a motor car from W. Black on credit for £5,000.

Analysis of transaction

Transaction	Ledger accounts	Classification of account	Increase or decrease	Recording instructions
Purchase of motor car on credit from W. Black	Motor car W. Black	Asset Liability	Increase Increase	Debit Credit

This transaction would be recorded in the ledger as follows:

DR.	Motor car a/c		CR.	DR.	W. Black a/c		CR.
	£					£	
W. Black	5,000				Motor car	5,000	

The ledger accounts have been shown in abbreviated form to keep the illustration simple.

Illustration

Recording a series of transactions using the double-entry system of bookkeeping

Assume that the following transactions take place:

1 January   A. Smith commences business with capital of £1,000 which he pays into the business bank account.
3 January   Goods bought by cheque for £300.
6 January   Goods sold for £150 and cheque received in settlement.
7 January   Shop fittings bought by cheque for £400.
8 January   Rent of £80 paid by cheque.

15

Analysis of transactions

Transaction	Ledger accounts	Classification of account	Increase or decrease	Recording instructions
Capital paid into bank	Bank Capital	Asset Capital	Increase Increase	Debit Credit
Purchases paid by cheque	Purchases Bank	Expense Asset	Increase Decrease	Debit Credit
Sales paid by cheque	Bank Sales	Asset Income	Increase Increase	Debit Credit
Shop fittings paid for by cheque	Fittings Bank	Asset Asset	Increase Decrease	Debit Credit
Rent paid for by cheque	Rent Bank	Expense Asset	Increase Decrease	Debit Credit

The entries in the ledger accounts would be as follows:

DR.	Bank a/c			CR.
	£			£
Jan 1 Capital	1,000	Jan 3 Purchases	300
6 Sales	150	7 Fittings	400
		8 Rent	80
		Balance	370
	1,150		1,150
9 Balance	370		

DR.	Capital a/c	CR.
		£
	Jan 1 Bank	1,000

DR.	Purchases a/c	CR.
	£	
Jan 3 Bank	300	

DR.	Sales a/c	CR.
		£
	Jan 6 Bank	150

DR.	Fittings a/c	CR.
	£	
Jan 7 Bank	400	

DR.	Rent a/c	CR.
	£	
Jan 8 Bank	80	

How to balance a ledger account

- ☐ It is usual to balance an account to find out the net increase or decrease in the account.
- ☐ The net increase or decrease is referred to as a balance.

Example of balance calculation

DR.			£	Bank a/c					CR. £
Jan	1	Capital	1,000	Jan	3	Purchases		⬆	300
	6	Sales	150		7	Fittings	③		400
					8	Rent		⬇	80
						Balance	① ④		370
			② 1,150						1,150
Jan	9	Balance	⑤ 370						

Procedure to be adopted in balancing an account

Step 1 Leave space for the balance on the side which has the smaller total.

Step 2 Add the side with the larger total and insert total.

Step 3 Add the column with the smaller total.

Step 4 Subtract the smaller from the greater total and insert the balance in the space left in Step 1.

Step 5 Bring down the balance on the opposite side of the account.

What is a folio?
- A folio is the page reference in an accounting book.
- The use of folios enables entries to be easily traced from one accounting record to another.
- The use of folios is possible if each ledger account in the ledger, and all pages in other accounting records, are assigned different numbers but kept in numerical order.
- A folio is entered against each entry in any accounting book which relates to the book from which it has been posted.

What is posting?
- The transfer of an entry from one account or other accounting record to another is known as *posting*.
- The operation of posting is necessary to meet the principle of the double-entry bookkeeping system.

Illustration *The use of folios and the operation of posting*

Assume A. Smith pays rent of £100 by cheque.

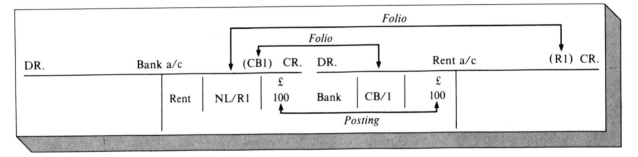

NL/R1 means nominal ledger, account no. R1.
CB/1 means cash book, page 1.

What is a trial balance?

☐ A trial balance consists of all the balances extracted from the ledger and arranged in two columns which are headed 'Debit' and 'Credit'.

☐ The objective of preparing a trial balance is to test the accuracy of the entries made in the ledger accounts.

☐ If the double-entry principle has been correctly applied both columns of the trial balance will be in agreement.

Illustration

The use of a trial balance as a means of checking the accuracy of entries made in the accounts

Using the same entries and accounts as in the example on **page 16**, the trial balance will appear thus:

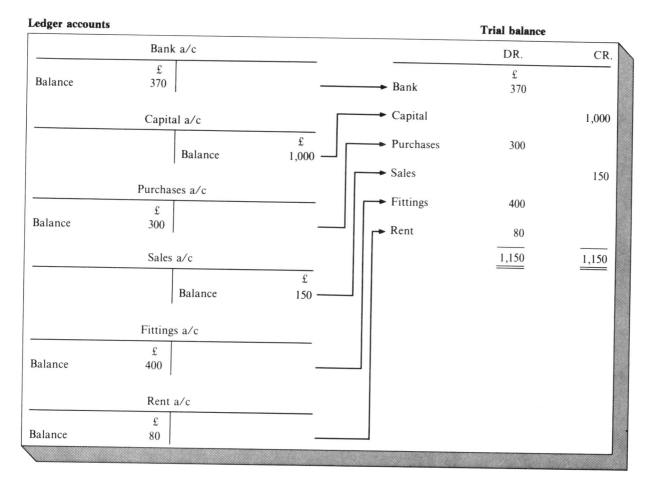

The trial balance is discussed in more detail in Chapter 11.

How to sectionalise the ledger

- ☐ It is necessary for control purposes to classify ledger accounts under main sections in many businesses.
- ☐ If the ledgers are sectionalised then it is possible to delegate responsibility for the writing up of these sections to different members of staff.
- ☐ If any form of computerisation of the accounting records is being introduced then the ledgers require to be sectionalised to obtain the full benefit of this system of accounting.

Main sections of the ledger

Sections	*Contents*
Bank cash book	All amounts paid by cheque and all income paid into the bank account
Petty cash book	All cash payments and amounts transferred from the bank cash book for petty cash payments
Sales (or debtors) ledger	All personal accounts of customers
Purchases (or creditors) ledger	All personal accounts of suppliers
Nominal ledger	All other accounts

Note 1   The bank cash book and petty cash book are considered as ledgers as well as being books of original entry.

Note 2   The nominal ledger is sometimes referred to as the impersonal ledger, general ledger or private ledger.

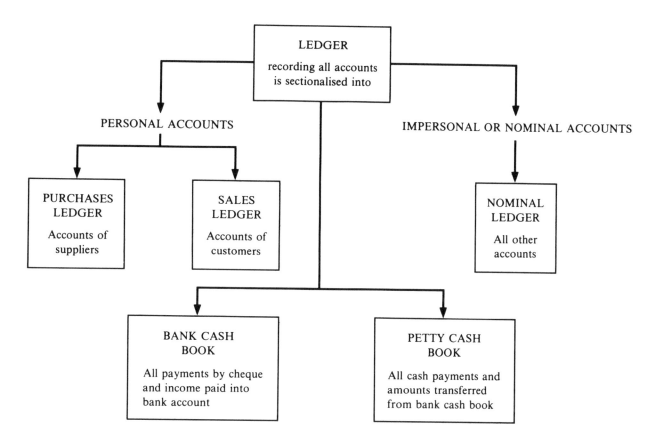

Books of original entry

It is a basic principle in accounting that one aspect of every transaction must be recorded through a book of original entry before it is posted to the sales, purchases or nominal ledgers. The books of original entry and their contents are as follows:

Book	Contents
Bank cash book	All payments made by cheque and all income which is paid into the bank account
Petty cash book	All cash payments and amounts transferred from the bank cash book for petty cash purposes
Purchases day book	Details of purchases made on credit from suppliers
Purchases returns book	Details of all returns to suppliers
Sales day book	Details of all credit sales to customers
Sales returns book	Details of all returns from customers
Journal	Details of transactions or adjustments that are not recorded in any other book of original entry

Note Although the bank cash book and petty cash book are considered to be ledgers they do form part of the books of original entry.

Books of original entry

Source document for writing up these books

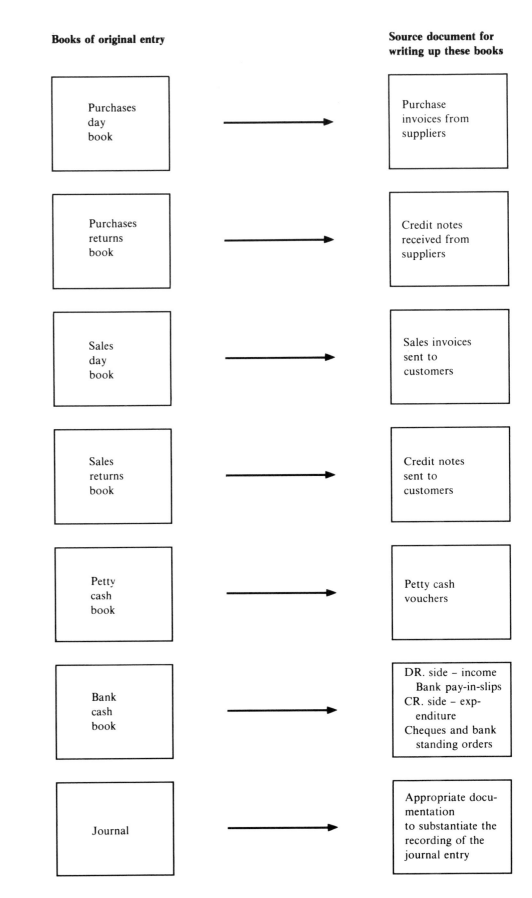

Books of original entry	Source document for writing up these books
Purchases day book	Purchase invoices from suppliers
Purchases returns book	Credit notes received from suppliers
Sales day book	Sales invoices sent to customers
Sales returns book	Credit notes sent to customers
Petty cash book	Petty cash vouchers
Bank cash book	DR. side – income Bank pay-in-slips CR. side – expenditure Cheques and bank standing orders
Journal	Appropriate documentation to substantiate the recording of the journal entry

What is a trading account?

Purpose

This account is concerned with setting the cost of goods sold against the amount received from the sale of goods. The difference between the amounts is termed gross profit.

Structure of a trading account

A. SMITH		
Trading account for year ended 31 December		
	£	£
SALES		40,000
Less: Cost of sales		
Purchases	15,000	
Add: Opening stock	5,000	
	20,000	
Less: Closing stock	7,000	13,000
GROSS PROFIT		27,000

The following points should be noted in connection with this account:

☐ Sales and purchases returns are usually deducted from the sales and purchases amounts before being recorded in the trading account.
☐ Although the above trading account has been shown in a vertical form it is still a ledger account and may be shown in the two-sided account style.
☐ Carriage inwards is usually shown as an item in the trading account if it refers to carriage on purchases.
☐ The trading account is compiled by transfers from the ledger accounts at the end of an accounting period, e.g.

Purchases a/c				Sales a/c			
	£		£		£		£
Balance	15,000	Trading	15,000	Trading	40,000	Balance	40,000

What is a profit and loss account?

Purpose

This account is concerned with setting off expenses from the gross profit and other sources of income. The difference is termed *net profit*.

Structure of a profit and loss account

A. SMITH
Profit and loss account for year ended 31 December

		£
Gross profit		27,000
Add: Income		
Discount received		100
Rents received		1,000
		28,100

		£	
Less: Expenses			
Office salaries		7,000	
Stationery and printing		500	
Telephone		300	
Rent and rates		600	
Heat and light		750	
Repairs to property		170	
Bad debts		30	
Discount allowed		50	
Salesmen's salaries and expenses		10,300	
Advertising		550	
Carriage outwards		250	
Depreciation on delivery vehicles		800	21,300
NET PROFIT			6,800

The following points should be noted in connection with this account:

- The account is shown in vertical form. Nevertheless, it is still a ledger account and may be shown in the traditional two-sided style.
- The gross profit is a transfer from the trading account.
- The profit and loss account is compiled by transfers from ledger accounts at the end of the accounting period, e.g.

Discount received a/c				Office salaries a/c		
	£		£		£		£
Profit and loss	100	Balance	100	Balance	7,000	Profit and loss	7,000

Structure of an analysed profit and loss account

A. SMITH			
Profit and loss account for year ended 31 December			
			£
Gross profit			27,000
Add: Income			
Discount received			100
Rents received			1,000
			28,100
Less: Expenses			
	£	£	
Administration			
Office salaries	7,000		
Stationery and printing	500		
Telephone	300	7,800	
Establishment			
Rent and rates	600		
Heat and light	750		
Repairs to property	170	1,520	
Financial			
Bad debts	30		
Discount allowed	50	80	
Selling and Distribution			
Salesmen's salaries and expenses	10,300		
Advertising	550		
Carriage outwards	250		
Depreciation on delivery vehicles	800	11,900	21,300
NET PROFIT			6,800

The advantage of analysing the profit and loss account in this way is that main headings of cost can be highlighted and compared with previous years to determine the amount of increase or decrease in each group of costs and so enable an element of cost control to be introduced into the business.

What is a manufacturing account?

Purpose

This account is concerned with the costs involved in producing goods where a business is engaged in the manufacturing process.

Basic elements of a manufacturing account

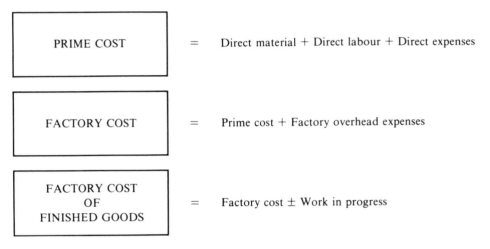

| PRIME COST | = | Direct material + Direct labour + Direct expenses |

| FACTORY COST | = | Prime cost + Factory overhead expenses |

| FACTORY COST OF FINISHED GOODS | = | Factory cost ± Work in progress |

Structure of a manufacturing account

A. SMITH
Manufacturing account for year ended 31 December

	£	£
Direct materials		
Purchases of raw materials	15,000	
Add: Opening stock	3,000	
	18,000	
Less: Closing stock	4,000	
	14,000	
Add: Carriage on raw materials	1,500	15,500
Direct wages		18,000
Direct expenses		500
PRIME COST		34,000
Factory overhead expenses		
Fuel and power	1,000	
Rent and rates	1,500	
Indirect wages	3,000	
Depreciation of plant	800	6,300
FACTORY COST		40,300
Adjustment for work in progress		
Opening valuation	2,500	
Closing valuation	3,700	1,200
FACTORY COST OF FINISHED GOODS		39,100

The following points should be noted in connection with this account:

- ☐ The above account has been shown in columnar form for ease of understanding. Nevertheless it is still a ledger account and may be shown in the traditional two-sided account style.
- ☐ The factory cost of finished goods is transferred to the trading account.
- ☐ Direct costs are costs that can be readily identified to the particular unit of goods being manufactured.
- ☐ Factory overhead expenses are expenses that are incurred in the factory but cannot be easily identified with the units being produced.
- ☐ Work-in-progress is the amount of uncompleted work in hand at the end of an accounting period.
- ☐ The manufacturing account is compiled by transfers from the ledger accounts at the end of the accounting period, e.g.

DR.	Raw materials a/c		CR.	DR.	Fuel and power a/c		CR.
	£		£		£		£
Balance	15,000	Manufacturing	15,000	Balance	1,000	Manufacturing	1,000

What is a balance sheet?

Purpose

This statement is prepared to show the nature and amount of the assets, liabilities and capital of the business at a given date.

Elements of a balance sheet

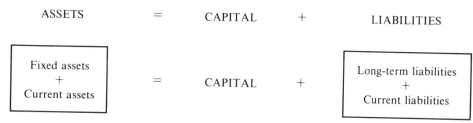

ASSETS	=	CAPITAL	+	LIABILITIES
Fixed assets + Current assets	=	CAPITAL	+	Long-term liabilities + Current liabilities

Observations on the balance sheet

- ☐ The balance sheet is a financial statement prepared as at a given date.
- ☐ The balance sheet is not a ledger account but a statement of balances classified under main headings.
- ☐ If prepared on a two-sided basis, the capital and liabilities show where the money has come from and the assets side shows how the money has been used.
- ☐ The owner's capital represents the net worth of the business.
- ☐ The net profit calculated in the profit and loss account is added to the owner's capital account.

Structure of a balance sheet

Two-sided presentation

A. SMITH
Balance sheet as at 31 December

	£	£		£	£
CAPITAL			FIXED ASSETS		
At start of year	28,000		Buildings	20,000	
Add: Profit for year	6,400		Plant	3,000	
	34,400		Motor vehicles	5,000	28,000
Less: Drawings	6,000	28,400	CURRENT ASSETS		
			Stock	6,000	
LONG-TERM LIABILITIES			Debtors	5,350	
Mortgage		5,000	Cash in hand	50	11,400
CURRENT LIABILITIES					
Creditors	4,000				
Bank overdraft	2,000	6,000			
		39,400			39,400

Vertical presentation

A. SMITH
Balance sheet as at 31 December

Ref.		£	£	£
1	FIXED ASSETS			
2	Buildings		20,000	
2	Plant		3,000	
2	Motor vehicles		5,000	28,000
3	CURRENT ASSETS			
4	Stock	6,000		
5	Debtors	5,350		
6	Cash in hand	50	11,400	
7	*Less:* CURRENT LIABILITIES			
8	Creditors	4,000		
9	Bank overdraft	2,000	6,000	5,400
				33,400
	Represented by:			
10	CAPITAL			
	At start of year		28,000	
11	*Add:* Profit for year		6,400	
			34,400	
12	*Less:* Drawings		6,000	28,400
13	LONG-TERM LIABILITIES			
14	Mortgage			5,000
				33,400

Key to vertical presentation

Ref.	Item	Description	Source
1	Fixed assets	These are amounts which are held permanently in the business and not for resale	Nominal ledger
2	Buildings, plant, motor vehicles	These are examples of fixed assets	Nominal ledger

Building a/c

	£
Balance	20,000

Plant a/c

	£
Balance	3,000

Motor vehicles a/c

	£
Balance	5,000

Ref.	Item	Description	Source
3	Current assets	These assets are constantly changing or circulating in the normal course of business	Sales and nominal ledgers, bank cash book and petty cash book
4	Stock	This is the value of stock held in the business at the end of the accounting period	Nominal ledger

Stock a/c

	£
Balance	6,000

Ref.	Item	Description	Source
5	Debtors	The total amount owed by customers	The total of the debtors' balances in the sales ledger
6	Cash in hand	The balance of cash in hand at the end of the accounting period	Petty cash book
7	Current liabilities	Liabilities that are currently due for payment normally less than one year from the balance sheet date	Purchases and nominal ledgers and bank cash book
8	Creditors	The total amount due to suppliers	The total of the creditors' balances in the purchases ledger
9	Bank overdraft	The sum due to the bank	Bank cash book
10	Capital	The amount due to the owner of the business	Nominal ledger

Capital a/c

	£		£
Drawings	6,000	Balance	28,000
Balance	28,400	Profit	6,400
	34,400		34,400

Ref.	Item	Description	Source
11	Profit	The net profit transferred from profit and loss account	Nominal ledger

Profit and loss a/c

	£		£
Capital	6,400	Balance	6,400

Ref.	Item	Description	Source
12	Drawings	The amount withdrawn by the owner for his personal use	Nominal ledger

Drawings a/c

	£		£
Balance	6,000	Capital	6,000

Ref.	Item	Description	Source
13	Long-term liabilities	These are loans and other liabilities due for repayment more than one year after the balance sheet date	Nominal ledger
14	Mortgage	This is the amount due to the mortgage company	Nominal ledger

Mortgage a/c

		£
	Balance	5,000

3 What is Capital and Revenue Expenditure?

What is capital expenditure?

- □ Expenditure incurred in acquiring assets of a permanent nature.
- □ Expenditure incurred where its benefits extend over one or more accounting periods.
- □ Expenditure of this type forms the fixed assets of the business and appears in the balance sheet.

Types of capital expenditure

Land and buildings, plant and machinery, furniture and fittings, motor vehicles, additions and extensions to fixed assets, installation of fixed assets, etc.

Revenue expenditure

- □ Expenditure incurred in servicing and maintaining fixed assets.
- □ Expenditure incurred when the benefits do not extend beyond the accounting period in which it takes place.
- □ Expenditure incurred in producing, selling and distributing the goods and services of the business together with the administrative expenses of running the business.
- □ Expenditure of this type appears in the profit and loss account.

Types of revenue expenditure

Purchases for resale, wages, salaries, rent, rates, telephone, electricity, bad debts, motor expenses, discount allowed, repairs and renewals, etc.

Distinction between capital and revenue expenditure

- □ The main distinction is one of permanence.
- □ It is essential to distinguish between capital and revenue expenditure if a true and correct profit is to be calculated.
- □ Revenue profit is calculated by deducting all revenue expenditure for the period from gross trading income.
- □ If capital expenditure is charged against revenue expenditure then the profit will be incorrectly reduced.
- □ Capital expenditure can only be written off in the profit and loss account in the form of depreciation.

Illustration

Problem

Allocate the following items of expenditure between capital and revenue expenditure and give reasons for the allocation:

		£
1	Purchase of lathe	5,000
2	Cost of installing lathe	500
3	Purchase of motor van	4,000
4	Cost of lettering the firm's name on van	200
5	Plant repairs	1,000
6	Purchase of patent rights	2,000
7	Cost of partitioning offices	1,700
8	Painting existing offices	500

Solution

Item	Nature of expenditure	Reason
1	Capital	Fixed asset
2	Capital	Additional cost to fixed asset
3	Capital	Fixed asset
4	Capital	Part of cost of fixed asset
5	Revenue	Maintenance of fixed asset
6	Capital	Fixed asset
7	Capital	Additional fixed asset
8	Revenue*	Maintenance of fixed asset

Note If this had been painting costs incurred in a new building the cost would have been treated as Capital since it would have been considered to be part of the cost of the new building.

Part 2 How to Set Up Your Bookkeeping System

4 How to Record Transactions Made by Cash or Cheque

Purpose To record receipts and payments of money by cash or cheque in a bank cash book.

Structure of the bank cash book The bank cash book described in this section has two sides: a debit side and a credit side.

Illustration *The debit side*

This records receipts of money from customers and other sources by cash or cheque, e.g. cash sales, cash or cheque payments from customers and other income such as interest, commission, dividends, etc. A column is included to record any discount allowed to customers.

Example of a ruling of the debit side of a bank cash book where analysis columns are used

Date	Details	Folio	Total	Discount	Sales ledger	Cash sales	Other income	VAT

Note 1: If the business is registered for VAT, an additional column should be included to record the VAT on any receipt of money except that included in any item shown in sales ledger column.
Note 2 The sales ledger column is reserved for all receipts from customers who have an account in the sales ledger. The amounts recorded will be inclusive of VAT.

The credit side

This records payments to suppliers for all goods and services by cheque, e.g. payments to creditors by cheque for goods for resale and payments for other expenditure such as telephone, rates, salaries and electricity. A column is included to record any discount received from suppliers.

Example of a ruling of the credit side of a bank cash book where analysis columns are used

Date	Details	Folio	Total	Discount	Purchases ledger	Other expenditure	VAT

Note 1 If the business is registered for VAT, an additional column should be included to record the VAT on any payment except that included in any item shown in the purchases ledger column.
Note 2 The purchases ledger column is reserved for all payments made to suppliers who have an account in the purchases ledger. The amounts recorded will be inclusive of VAT.
Note 3 In the above example, only one column has been shown for other expenditure. This may be inadequate for many businesses and it may be necessary to include other analysis columns for electricity, salaries, printing, etc.
Note 4 In this example of the bank cash book, only payments made by cheque are recorded on the credit side. Any payments in cash must be shown in the Petty Cash Book (see page 45).

Illustration   *Bank cash book with no analysis columns*

A. SMITH   Folio CBI

DR.				BANK CASH BOOK			CR.
Date	Details	Folio	Amount	Date	Details	Folio	Amount
			£				£
Jan 1	Balance	b/d	500	Jan 3	W. Brown ④ (Ch. 123)	PL/B2	60
3	T. Smith ①	SL/S4	50	5	Electricity ⑤ (Ch. 124)	NL/E2	15
	Cash sales ②	NL/S1	20	7	Rates (Ch. 125) ⑥	NL/R1	30
5	Dividend ③	NL/D2	5	12	Bank charges ⑦	NL/B6	6
				14	Sub. AA ⑧ (Standing order)	NL/S3	25
				31	Balance	c/d	439
			575				575
Feb 1	Balance	b/d	439				

Bank statement recording the above transactions in the bank cash book

A. Smith: Bank statement for January

Date	Details	DR.	CR.	Balance
		£	£	£
Jan 1	Balance			500
4	Lodgment		70	570
5	Cheque	123	60	510
	Dividend from investment		5	515
8	Cheque	124	15	500
10	Cheque	125	30	470
12	Bank charges for period		6	464
14	Sub. AA standing order		25	439

Note 1   The lodgment of £70 is made up of the two amounts received by the business on 3 January, *viz.* cheque from T. Smith, £50, and cash sales, £20.

Note 2   The dates of the transactions included in the bank statement are different from those shown in the bank cash book. This is caused by the time lag in the receipt of lodgments by the bank and presentation of cheques for payment to the bank. (For further information on bank statements, see page 90.)

Illustration   *Pay-in-slip relating to lodgement on 3 January 19X1*

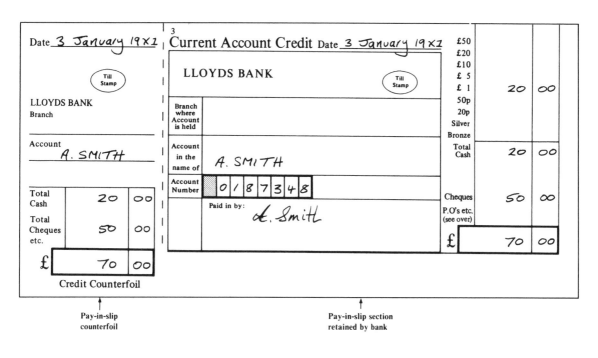

Note: Only the total of cheques received is listed on the above counterfoil, but paying-in books can be obtained with space for listing cheques individually.

Illustration   *Cheque paid to W. Brown on 3 January 19X1*

Section of cheque sent to W. Brown

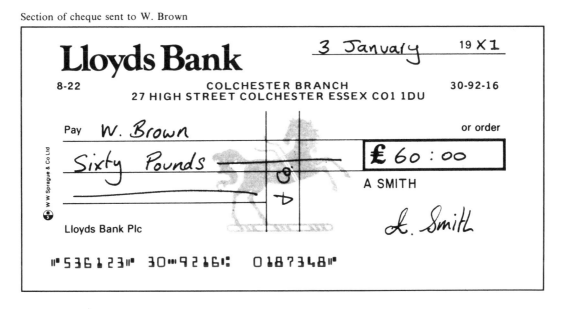

Note: Counterfoils are not provided with the above type of cheque. Amounts can be listed in the front of the cheque book.

Analysis of transactions shown in bank cash book

	Ref.	Transaction			Source document for writing up bank cash book
Receipts	1	Jan	3	Received a cheque amounting to £50 from T. Smith a credit customer of the business	Cheque from customer
	2	Jan	3	Cash sales amounted to £20	Total of till roll
	3	Jan	5	Dividend received from investment	Dividend counterfoil/entry on bank statement
Payments	4	Jan	3	Paid to W. Brown by cheque £60	Invoice and/or statement from creditor
	5	Jan	5	Payment of electricity bill by cheque for £15	Account from electricity board
	6	Jan	7	Paid rates by cheque £30	Rates notice
	7	Jan	12	Bank charges for period	Bank statement
	8	Jan	14	Sub. paid to AA by standing order £25	Copy of standing order lodged with bank

How to Record Transactions Made by Cash or Cheque

Treatment for banking	Recording instructions	How corresponding entries appear in ledger accounts
Lodged in bank through pay-in-slip (see example)	DR. Bank cash book CR. T. Smith a/c in sales ledger	**SALES LEDGER** Folio S4 DR.　　　　T. Smith a/c　　　　CR. 　　　　　　　　　　　　　　£ Jan　3　Bank CB/1　　50
Lodged in bank through pay-in-slip (see example)	DR. Bank cash book CR. Sales a/c in nominal ledger	**NOMINAL LEDGER** Folio S1 DR.　　　　Cash sales a/c　　　　CR. 　　　　　　　　　　　　　　£ Jan　3　Bank CB/1　　20
Dividend was paid direct to bank	DR. Bank cash book CR. Dividend a/c in nominal ledger	**NOMINAL LEDGER** Folio D2 DR.　　　　Dividend a/c　　　　CR. 　　　　　　　　　　　　　　£ Jan　5　Bank CB/1　　5
Cheque (see example)	DR. W. Brown a/c in purchases ledger CR. Bank cash book	**PURCHASES LEDGER** Folio B2 DR.　　　　W. Brown a/c　　　　CR. 　　　　　　　　£ Jan　3　Bank CB/1　60
Cheque	DR. Electricity a/c in nominal ledger CR. Bank cash book	**NOMINAL LEDGER** Folio E2 DR.　　　　Electricity a/c　　　　CR. 　　　　　　　　£ Jan　5　Bank CB/1　15
Cheque	DR. Rates a/c in nominal ledger CR. Bank cash book	**NOMINAL LEDGER** Folio R1 DR.　　　　Rates a/c　　　　CR. 　　　　　　　£ Jan　7　Bank CB/1　30
Bank has debited the bank account with amount of bank charges	DR. Bank charges a/c in nominal ledger CR. Bank cash book	**NOMINAL LEDGER** Folio B6 DR.　　　　Bank charges a/c　　　　CR. 　　　　　　　£ Jan　12　Bank CB/1　6
Bank has paid the AA direct and debited the bank account	DR. Subscriptions a/c in nominal ledger CR. Bank cash book	**NOMINAL LEDGER** Folio S3 DR.　　　　Subscriptions a/c　　　　CR. 　　　　　　　£ Jan　14　Bank CB/1　25

Note The balances shown at the beginning and end of the month represent the amount of cash at bank on those dates.

Analysed bank cash book

Advantages

- ☐ Provides details of individual amounts of income banked and analysis of payments recorded in separate columns.
- ☐ Reduces the number of postings to the nominal ledger since only the total column of each income and expense heading is posted once a month to the nominal ledger.

Illustration

Using the information in the previous example, the bank cash book can be converted into an analysed bank cash book in the following way:

Bank cash book: receipts side
Folio CB1

Date	Details	Folio	Total	Sales ledger	Cash sales	Dividends
			£	£	£	£
Jan 1	Balance	b/d	500			
3	T. Smith	SL/S4	50	50		
	Cash sales		20		20	
5	Dividend		5			5
			575	50	20	5
					NL/S1	NL/D2

Note 1 Additional columns could be added as appropriate for the requirements of the business.
Note 2 The transactions to be posted to the nominal ledger would not be posted individually, but in total at the end of the month.
Note 3 Each amount received from a debtor would require to be posted to the debtor's account in the sales ledger on an individual basis.

Bank cash book: payments side
Folio CB1

Date	Details	Folio	Total	Purchases ledger	Electricity	Rates	Bank charges	Subscriptions
			£	£	£	£	£	£
Jan 3	W. Brown	PL/B2	60	60				
5	Electricity		15		15			
7	Rates		30			30		
12	Bank charges		6				6	
14	Sub. – AA		25					25
31	Balance	c/d	439					
			575	60	15	30	6	25
					NL/E2	NL/R1	NL/B6	NL/S3

Note 1 Additional columns could be added as appropriate for the requirements of the business.
Note 2 The transactions to be posted to the nominal ledger would not be posted individually, but in total at the end of the month.
Note 3 Each amount paid to a creditor would require to be posted to the creditor's account in the purchases ledger on an individual basis.

Analysed bank cash book with discount and VAT columns

Purpose

To illustrate the recording of receipts and payments in an analysed bank cash book with discount columns included.

Problem

T. Jack has a balance of £1,000 at the bank on 1 January and makes the following transactions during the month of January. Before recording the transactions they have been grouped together under main headings.

Receipts

Cash sales

	Ex. VAT	VAT
Jan 14	£300	£45
28	260	39

Payments received from debtors

		Cheque received	Discount allowed
Jan 12	B. Brown	£200	£5
17	A. Green	100	3
20	W. Black	50	—

Commission received from agency sales

	Ex. VAT	VAT
Jan 21	£60	£9

Payments

Payments made to creditors

		Cheque paid	Discount received
Jan 14	T. Smith	£400	£20
21	A. Knox	95	—
28	B. Thom	310	15

Payment made in respect of telephone charges

		Ex. VAT	VAT
Jan 26	Cheque	£40	£6

Amounts drawn for petty cash

Jan 15	Cheque	£30
30	Cheque	£50

Payments made for travelling expenses

Jan 8	British Rail	£55
10	British Airways	£110

Payments made for general expenses

Jan 12	Cheque	£16
20	Cheque	£5

Solution

Bank cash book: receipts side

Folio CB1

Date	Details	Folio	Total	Discount	Sales ledger	Cash sales	Commission	VAT
			£	£	£	£	£	£
Jan 1	Balance	b/d	1,000					
12	B. Brown	SL/B1	200	5	200			
14	Cash sales		345			300		45
17	A. Green	SL/G2	100	3	100			
20	W. Black	SL/B3	50		50			
21	Commission		69				60	9
28	Cash sales		299			260		39
			2,063	8	350	560	60	93
				NL/D3	NL/S4	NL/S4	NL/C2	NL/V1

DR. VAT a/c Folio V1 CR.
£
Jan 31 Total CB/1 93
per
CB

DR. Commission a/c Folio C2 CR.
£
Jan 31 Total CB/1 60
per
CB

DR. Discount a/c Folio D3 CR.
£
Jan 31 Total CB/1 8
from
CB

DR. Cash sales a/c Folio S4 CR.
£
Jan 31 Total CB/1 560
per
CB

POSTINGS TO SALES LEDGER

DR. B. Brown a/c Folio B1 CR.
£
Jan 12 Bank CB/1 200
Discount CB/1 5
205

DR. A. Green a/c Folio G2 CR.
£
Jan 17 Bank CB/1 100
Discount CB/1 3
103

DR. W. Black a/c Folio B3 CR.
£
Jan 20 Bank CB/1 50

Bank cash book: payments side

Folio CB1

Date	Details	Folio	Total	Discount	Purchases ledger	Petty cash	Telephone	Travel expenses	General expenses	VAT
			£	£	£	£	£	£	£	£
Jan 8	British Rail		55					55		
10	British Airways		110					110		
12	General expenses		16						16	
14	T. Smith	PL/S4	400	20	400					
15	Petty cash		30			30				
20	General expenses		5						5	
21	A. Knox	PL/K1	95		95					
26	Telephone		46				40			6
28	B. Thom	PL/T3	310	15	310					
30	Petty cash		50			50				
			1,117	35	805	80	40	165	21	6
31	Balance	c/d	946							
			2,063							
				NL/D3		PCB/1	NL/T3	NL/T4	NL/G6	NL/V1

Folio V1

DR.   VAT a/c   CR.
£
Jan 31   Total   CB/1   6
from CB

Folio G6

DR.   General expenses a/c   CR.
£
Jan 31   Total   CB/1   21
from CB

Folio T4

DR.   Travel expenses a/c   CR.
£
Jan 31   Total   CB/1   165
from CB

Folio D3

DR.   Discount a/c   CR.
£
Jan 31   Total   CB/1   35
from CB

Folio PCB1

DR.   Petty cash book   CR.
£
Jan 31   Total   CB/1   80
from CB

Folio T3

DR.   Telephone a/c   CR.
£
Jan 31   Total   CB/1   40
from CB

POSTINGS TO PURCHASES LEDGER

Folio S4

DR.   T. Smith a/c   CR.
£
Jan 14   Bank   CB/1   400
       Discount CB/1   20
                420

Folio K1

DR.   A. Knox a/c   CR.
£
Jan 21   Bank   CB/1   95

Folio T3

DR.   B. Thom a/c   CR.
£
Jan 28   Bank   CB/1   310
       Discount CB/1   15
                325

Notes on solution

Receipts side

Column	Comments
Total	This column includes the opening and/or closing balances on the bank cash book.
	The amounts shown in the total column are the actual amounts received by the business, including VAT, but excluding discount.
	Under the bank cash book system all amounts received must be lodged in the bank whether received in cash or by cheque.
Discount	This is purely a memorandum column for the recording of discount allowed to debtors and does not affect the bank balance.
	The amount of discount is not included in the total column.
	The discount allowed is posted to the debtor's account (see posting instructions sales ledger column).
Sales ledger	This column is reserved for the payments received from debtors who have an account in the sales ledger.
	The total of this column is not posted to any account in the nominal ledger but the total is used for sales ledger control purposes.
	If discount is allowed to any debtor the amount of discount is posted to the debtor's account together with the payment received.
Cash sales and commission	The amount of cash sales and commission received are entered ex VAT.
VAT	This column is reserved for the VAT included in all sums received with the exception of sums received which have been entered in the sales ledger column.

Filing of source documents

Receipts side of bank cash book

The following documents should be filed in order of receipt and reference made to the bank cash book:
  Pay-in-slips
  Till roll slips
  Copy receipts issued to customers
  Dividend counterfoils and documentation relating to other sources of income

Payments side of bank cash book

The following documents should be filed in order of payment and reference made to the bank cash book:
  Paid cheques, if available, and/or with cheque counterfoils.
  Appropriate receipts issued by creditors and for services rendered such as telephone and electricity accounts. These receipts should be attached to the appropriate paid cheque if available.
Bank statements supplied by the bank should also be filed in date order after they have been checked with the bank cash book.

Payments side

Column	Comments
Total	This column includes the opening and/or closing balances on the bank cash book.
	The amounts shown in the total column are the actual amounts paid by the business, including VAT, but excluding discount received.
	Under the bank cash book system all amounts paid must be by cheque.
Discount	This is purely a memorandum column for the recording of discount received from creditors and does not affect the bank balance.
	The amount of discount is not included in the total column.
	The discount received is posted to the creditor's account (see posting instructions purchases ledger column).
Purchases ledger	This column is reserved for payments made to creditors who have an account in the purchases ledger.
	The total of this column is not posted to any account in the nominal ledger but the total is used for purchases ledger control purposes.
	If discount is received from any creditor the amount of discount is posted to the creditor's account together with the payment made.
Petty cash	The total of this column represents the amount drawn for petty cash and is transferred to the petty cash book.
Telephone, travel expenses and general expenses	The amounts paid in respect of telephone, travel and general expenses or any other type of expenditure are entered in the bank cash book ex VAT.
VAT	This column is reserved for the VAT included in all payments with the exception of amounts paid to creditors which have been entered in the purchases ledger column.

What is a petty cash book?

Purpose

The petty cash book is used for recording cash payments made by a business.

Advantages of using an analysed petty cash book

- ☐ All cash expenditure is recorded in one book. This facilitates the control of actual cash.
- ☐ The entries are easy to record and the book is capable of being written up by a junior member of the office staff.
- ☐ It is simple to post items of expenditure to the appropriate accounts in the nominal ledger when the petty cash book is written up in an analysed form.

Structure

The petty cash book has two sides:

Debit side   To record sums of cash transferred from the main bank cash book.

45

Credit side To record payments made in cash, e.g. postages, travelling expenses, cash purchases and sundry expenses of small amounts.

Example of petty cash book ruling

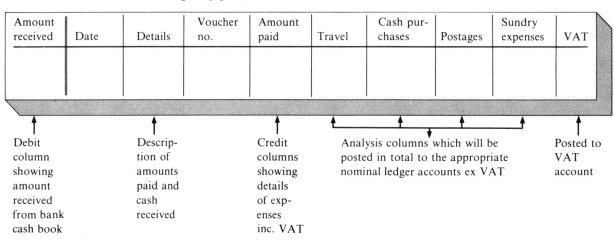

Amount received	Date	Details	Voucher no.	Amount paid	Travel	Cash purchases	Postages	Sundry expenses	VAT

Debit column showing amount received from bank cash book

Description of amounts paid and cash received

Credit columns showing details of expenses inc. VAT

Analysis columns which will be posted in total to the appropriate nominal ledger accounts ex VAT

Posted to VAT account

Note that if a business is registered for VAT, an additional column should be included to record the VAT on any payment in which there is an element of VAT. The number and the nature of the analysis will vary in each business.

Example of a petty cash voucher

	Petty Cash Voucher No. ___		
Date _____			
Details		£	p
Authorised signature _____			

A petty cash voucher should be completed and an authorisation signature obtained for every payment made in the petty cash book. Appropriate receipts where available should be attached to these vouchers. The vouchers should be referenced to the petty cash book and filed in date order.

Notes on illustration opposite

Column	Comment
Amount received	This represents the sum of cash transferred from the bank cash book.
Voucher no.	This refers to the petty cash voucher number. A petty cash voucher must be completed for each expense item.
Amount paid	This is total sum paid for each item of expenditure, including VAT.

Illustration *Recording receipts in an analysed petty cash book*

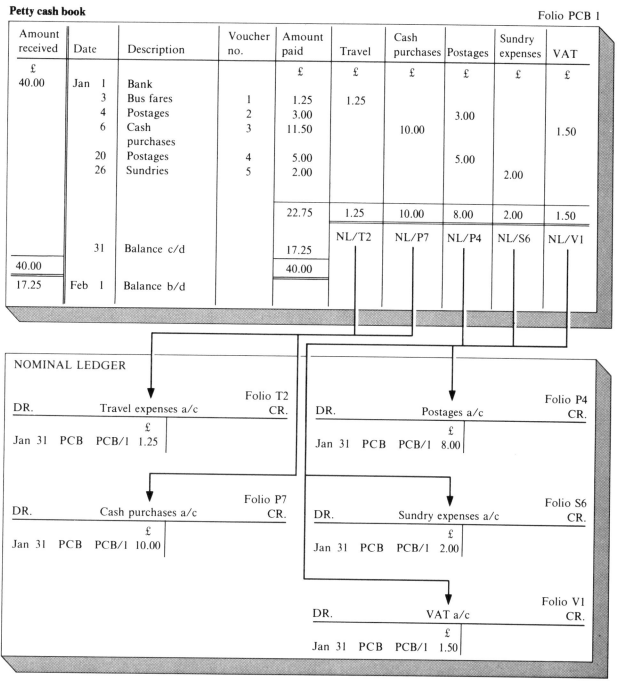

Petty cash book   Folio PCB 1

Amount received	Date	Description	Voucher no.	Amount paid	Travel	Cash purchases	Postages	Sundry expenses	VAT
£ 40.00	Jan 1	Bank		£	£	£	£	£	£
	3	Bus fares	1	1.25	1.25				
	4	Postages	2	3.00			3.00		
	6	Cash purchases	3	11.50		10.00			1.50
	20	Postages	4	5.00			5.00		
	26	Sundries	5	2.00				2.00	
				22.75	1.25	10.00	8.00	2.00	1.50
					NL/T2	NL/P7	NL/P4	NL/S6	NL/V1
	31	Balance c/d		17.25					
40.00				40.00					
17.25	Feb 1	Balance b/d							

NOMINAL LEDGER

DR. Travel expenses a/c Folio T2 CR.
£
Jan 31 PCB PCB/1 1.25

DR. Postages a/c Folio P4 CR.
£
Jan 31 PCB PCB/1 8.00

DR. Cash purchases a/c Folio P7 CR.
£
Jan 31 PCB PCB/1 10.00

DR. Sundry expenses a/c Folio S6 CR.
£
Jan 31 PCB PCB/1 2.00

DR. VAT a/c Folio V1 CR.
£
Jan 31 PCB PCB/1 1.50

	Column	Comment
(Continued from page 46)	Travel, cash purchases, postages and sundry expenses	These columns are referred to as analysis columns in which are recorded the various items of expenditure excluding VAT. The totals are posted to the appropriate accounts in the nominal ledger.
	VAT	This column is reserved for the VAT included in all payments and is posted in total to the VAT account at the end of each month.

5 How to Control and Record Credit Purchases

Method of purchasing goods on credit

□ A letter of enquiry is usually written by the business to a prospective supplier requesting a quotation for certain goods or services together with delivery dates.

□ If the quotation received is accepted, an official pre-numbered order form is completed and (after authorisation) sent to the supplier. Copies of the order should be sent to the ordering department and the accounting department.

□ When the goods are received they must be examined by the ordering department and checked against the order with the accompanying delivery note. A record of all goods delivered should be kept and cross-referenced to the order and delivery note. The goods are then entered on the stock record system.

□ On receipt of the invoice from the supplier it is checked against the order and the goods received book. Prices, extensions, additions, etc., are verified by the accounting staff.

□ After the invoices have been checked they are then recorded in the purchases day book and thereafter filed. The date and amount of each invoice recorded in the purchases day book is then posted to the supplier's account in the purchases ledger.

□ If goods are to be returned for any reason then an advice slip is prepared and sent to the supplier advising of the reason for returning the goods. A copy of this advice slip must be kept.

□ On acceptance of the returned goods the supplier will then send a credit note giving details of the goods returned and the amount of the allowance made to the business.

□ On receipt of the credit note it will be checked against the advice slip and then recorded in the purchases returns book and thereafter filed. The date and amount of each credit note recorded in the purchases returns book is then posted to the supplier's account in the purchases ledger.

□ The supplier will normally send a statement of account giving details of all invoices, credit notes and payments made in respect of the period covered by the statement, usually a month. After receiving the statement the business will then check the information contained therein with the supplier's account in the purchases ledger and, if found to be correct, then pass it for payment.

Important points to be observed when purchasing goods

□ Goods should be purchased from suppliers in sufficient quantities and at the best prices obtainable.

□ Authorisation for all goods purchased should be made by one person, or if a large business, through the ordering department.

□ Accurate records of all goods ordered should be kept so that they can be checked with goods received from suppliers.

Documents used for controlling and recording credit purchases

Letter of inquiry This is a letter sent by the business to a prospective supplier requesting prices, delivery dates, etc., of certain goods or services required by the business.

48

Quotation   This is a document sent by the supplier to the business, stating the price of goods and services, delivery date and the terms and conditions under which the goods will be sold.

Order   The order form (see page 50) is sent to the supplier by the business detailing the quantity, type and delivery date of goods or services required together with their quoted price. The order form should be numbered and copies kept by the business.

Advice note   This document is sent by the supplier to the business when the goods are despatched. Information on the quantity, type and date of despatch of the goods are included in this note. No information on the price of the goods is shown.

Delivery note   A delivery note usually accompanies the goods and shows similar information to that included in the advice note.

Invoice   This document (see page 51) is sent by the supplier to the business and gives details of the goods or services purchased and the amount due to be paid for them. Information on terms of payment such as cash discount is usually shown on the invoice. If the supplier is registered for VAT, their VAT number must be shown on the invoice.

Credit note   A credit note (see page 52) is sent by the supplier of goods or services to the business when a reduction of the amount charged on the invoice is to be made. This can occur when goods have been returned by the business as faulty, when an overcharge has been made on the invoice or when packing cases or containers have been charged on the invoice and subsequently returned by the business.

Statement   At the end of each month the supplier sends a statement (see page 53) to the business showing details of the business transactions that have taken place during the month and the amount due to be paid by the business to the supplier.

Chart of business transactions relating to credit purchases and credit sales

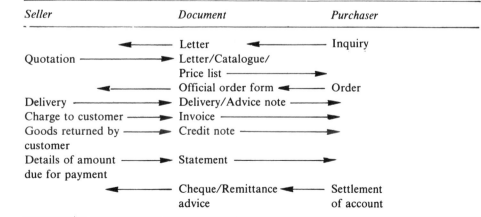

Example of purchase order form

PURCHASE ORDER				A. SMITH	

Registered No: 123456 England
Registered Office: Long Street, Bartown.

ELECTRICAL SUPPLIES
83 NEW ROAD,
ANYTOWN

					Order No.	
Date of Order		Date Required	Your Reference CS417	For queries please contact JR	**0651**	
Item	Quantity		Description			Price
	20		Standard Lamps			£500

White	Yellow	Pink	Please quote Order No. on delivery advice, invoice and other correspondence	For	A. SMITH
Purchase Order	Accounts Copy	Progress Copy			

Kalamazoo
BUSINESS SYSTEMS
29-800138-98

Example of purchase invoice

				0364
Invoice			**ELECTRICAL SUPPLIES**	

83 New Road, Anytown ANY 9LK

Telephone: ANY 5000 STD 0224 5000

Telegrams: Speeds Anytown

VAT No. 912 3456 87

A. SMITH
Long Street,
Bartown

Your Order No. 0651	Goods Sent Per BRS		Date Sent 6 Jan	Carriage Paid Home	Invoice Date (Tax Point) 6th January

Quantity	Description	Price	Amount VAT Rate 15 %	VAT Rate %	VAT Rate %
20	Standard Lamps	£25	£500		

INVOICE ALLOCATION

ANALYSIS	AMOUNT
LAMPS	£500
VAT	75

Kalamazoo
BUSINESS SYSTEMS
724530-98

Terms: Strictly Nett Monthly

Value ➡	£500		
VAT ➡	75		

SALE

Total Value £500	Total VAT £75	➡ £ 575.00
		AMOUNT OWING

Example of credit note

				83 New Road			0396

ELECTRICAL SUPPLIES

Authorised distributors of Anyproducts

83 New Road
Anytown
Anycounty ANY 9LK
Telephone: ANY 5000
Telegrams: Speeds Anytown

0396

VAT No. 912 3456 87

A. SMITH
Long Street,
Bartown.

Credit Note

Date   January 12th

Quantity	Description	Price	Amount VAT Rate 15 %	VAT Rate %	VAT Rate %
4	Standard Lamps	£25	£100		

CREDIT NOTE ALLOCATION

ANALYSIS	AMOUNT
LAMPS	£100
VAT	15

Reason for Credit	Returned Faulty	Value ➡	£100	
		VAT ➡	15	
	Original Invoice No. **0364** Dated 6 January			

Kalamazoo
BUSINESS SYSTEMS
29-757371-98

Total Value	Total VAT	➡ £115.00
£100	15	**Amount owing**

Example of statement

ELECTRICAL SUPPLIES		
Hardware Factors and General Wholesalers		

83 New Road
Anytown
England
Telephone: Any 500
Telegrams: Speeds England

⌐   A. SMITH
Long Street
Bartown ¬

└ ┘

Statement   Date 31 January

DATE	REF. NO.	DETAILS	VAT		DEBIT		CREDIT		BALANCE	
Jan 6	0364	Goods	75	00	500	00			575	00
12	0396	Returns	15	00			100	00	460	00

Last amount
in the balance
column is
amount owing

Kalamazoo P.10B 522185 7⅛x6⅞

53

Method of checking invoices from suppliers

On receipt of the invoice from the supplier the business should check on the following:

☐ The invoice is in agreement with the order form as regards price, quantities, VAT, etc.

☐ The invoice is correct arithmetically in respect of extensions and the total column.

☐ The goods or services included in the invoice have been received and are found to be in order.

☐ The invoice should be analysed under appropriate headings for recording purposes in the purchases day book (see analysed purchases day book).

Method of making payment of amounts due to suppliers

☐ The statement received from the supplier should be checked with the supplier's account in the purchases ledger to ensure that they are in agreement.

☐ If no statement is received then the amount due to the supplier will be the balance on their account in the purchases ledger. This should be verified against invoices and credit notes received from the supplier before payment is made.

☐ Check on terms of settlement. Deduct any discount if this is allowed by the supplier.

☐ Before paying any supplier ensure that there are sufficient funds in the bank to meet the payment.

☐ Write out the cheque for the amount of the payment. The cheque should be signed by the owner of the business, by a director, or by an authorised signatory in the case of a large business.

Method of recording credit purchases in the accounting records of the business

Purchases day book

☐ This is a book of original entry which records credit purchase transactions only.

☐ All purchase invoices are listed, analysed and summarised in this book.

☐ The name of each supplier, date of supply of goods or services and the amount to be credited to the supplier's account is shown in the purchases day book.

☐ The total of the purchases day book is posted to the purchases account assuming that all goods included in the purchases day book are for resale. If other credit purchases are included such as motor cars, stationery, etc., these are posted to the appropriate accounts in the nominal ledger.

Recording purchase invoices in the purchases day book and posting to the suppliers' accounts in the purchases ledger

Assume A. Smith makes the following credit purchases:

```
 3 January   Inv. 1   R. Brown supplies goods at £200
10 January   Inv. 2   W. Green supplies goods at £300
15 January   Inv. 3   A. Black supplies goods at £100
```

The procedure to be adopted in writing up the purchases day book is then as follows:

☐ Enter invoices in purchases day book in date order and reference them.
☐ Post the amount of each invoice to the credit of the supplier's account in the purchases ledger.
☐ Post the total of the purchases day book to the purchases account in the nominal ledger.

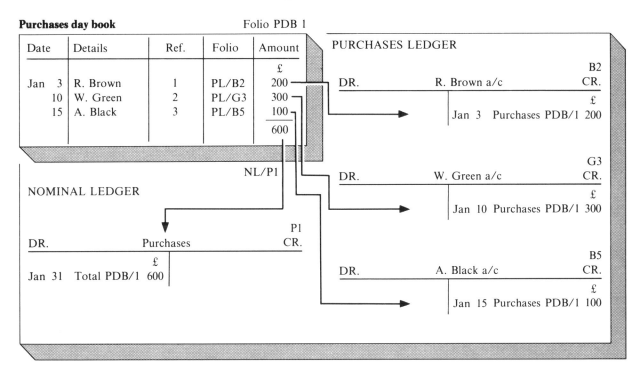

Purchases returns book

☐ This is a book of original entry in which details of credit notes sent by suppliers are recorded.
☐ All credit notes are listed, analysed and summarised in this book.
☐ The name of each supplier, date of credit note and amount thereof to be debited to the supplier's account is shown in the purchases returns book.
☐ The total of the purchases returns book is posted to the purchases returns account if all goods included in the purchases returns book are for resale. If other items are included such as stationery, packing, etc., these are posted to the appropriate accounts in the nominal ledger.

Recording credit notes in the purchases returns book and posting to the suppliers' accounts

Assume A. Smith receives the following credit notes from his suppliers:

15 January   CN1   R. Brown sent a credit note for £50
30 January   CN2   A. Black sent a credit note for £30

The procedure to be adopted in writing up the purchases returns book is then as follows:

□   Enter credit notes in the purchases returns book in date order and reference them.
□   Post the amount of each credit note to the debit of the supplier's account in the purchases ledger.
□   Post the total of the purchases returns book to the credit of the purchases returns account in the nominal ledger.

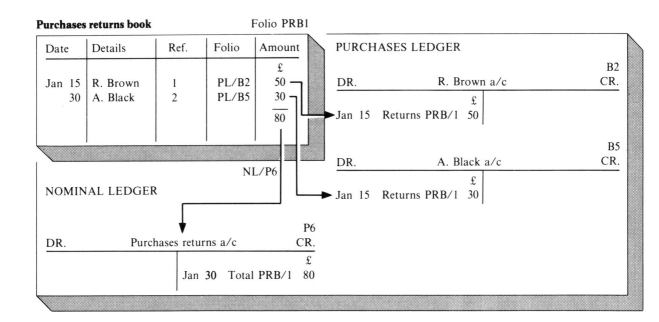

How to record payments to suppliers in the bank cash book and purchases ledger

Method to be adopted in recording payments to suppliers in the bank cash book and posting the amounts to the purchases ledger

□   Enter cheque payments to suppliers in the total column of the bank cash book credit side and extend the amount into the 'Purchases ledger' column.
□   If discount is allowed by supplier enter the amount of discount in the 'Discount' column against the appropriate cheque payment in bank cash book credit side.

☐ Post the cheque payment and the discount received from the bank cash book to the debit side of the supplier's account in the purchases ledger. The 'Discount' column in the bank cash book is posted to the credit of the discount account in the nominal ledger.

Assume for the sake of example that A. Smith pays the following amounts by cheque to his suppliers:

20 January   R. Brown payment £150
30 January   W. Green payment £290 (discount of £10 allowed on this payment)
31 January   A. Black payment £70

Then, using the information included in the previous examples relating to purchases and returns, the entries in the bank cash book and ledgers would appear thus:

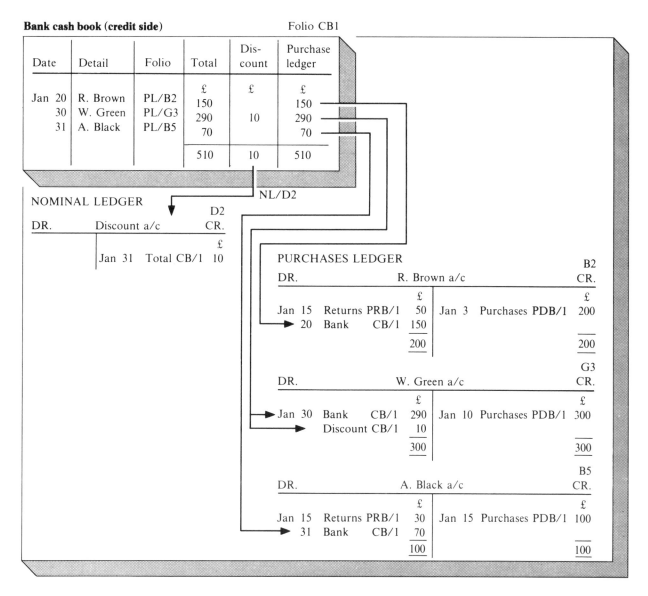

Analysed purchases day book

Advantages of using an analysed purchases day book

☐ Provides an analysis of purchases over departments or other sectional activities of the business.

☐ Assists in the calculation of profit earned in each activity of the business.

☐ Makes it easier to post the analysed amounts to the nominal ledger.

Recording invoices in analysed purchases day book

☐ Analyse each invoice in accordance with the analysis columns shown in the analysed purchases day book (see example below).

☐ Enter details of each invoice in date order in the analysed purchases day book recording the amount of each invoice in the total column.

☐ Extend the amount of each invoice to the appropriate analysis columns as analysed on the invoice.

☐ Post the total amount of each invoice to the credit of the supplier's account in the purchases ledger.

☐ Post the total of the analysis columns of the analysed purchases day book to the appropriate accounts in the nominal ledger.

Ruling of an analysed purchases day book

Date	Details	Ref.	Folio	Total	Tables	Carpets	Chairs	Lamps	VAT
				£	£	£		£	£
Jan 6	Electrical Supplies	1	PL/E2	575				500	75
20	New Furniture Company	2	PL/N1	5,750	5,000				750
25	Rug Company Ltd	3	PL/R1	1,150		1,000			150

Date of invoice — Name of supplier — Invoice no. — Supplier's account folio — Invoice total inc. VAT — Analysis columns which will be posted to the appropriate accounts in the nominal ledger ex VAT — Posted to VAT account

Illustration

Recording invoices including VAT in an analysed purchases day book and posting to the purchases ledger

Assume A. Smith has the following credit purchase transactions

6 January   Inv. 1   W. Fox supplied goods amounting to £400 + VAT £60, which were allocated as follows:
To Dept A   £100 + VAT £15
To Dept B   £300 + VAT £45

7 January   Inv. 2   F. Stone supplied goods amounting to £200 + VAT £30, which were allocated as follows:
To Dept A   £40 + VAT £6
To Dept B   £160 + VAT £24

21 January   Inv. 3   T. Gray supplied goods amounting to £600 + VAT £90, which were allocated as follows:
To Dept A   £100 + VAT £15
To Dept B   £500 + VAT £75

58

Purchases day book   Folio PDB1

Date	Details	Ref.	Folio	Total	Dept A	Dept B	Fittings	VAT
				£	£	£	£	£
Jan 6	W. Fox	1	PL/F2	460	100	300		60
7	F. Stone	2	PL/S3	230	40	160		30
21	T. Gray	3	PL/G6	690	100		500	90
				1,380	240	460	500	180
					NL/P1	NL/P2	NL/F1	NL/V1

PURCHASES LEDGER

DR.   W. Fox a/c   F2 CR.

				£
Jan 6	Purchases PDB/1	460

DR.   F. Stone a/c   S3 CR.

				£
Jan 7	Purchases PDB/1	230

DR.   T. Gray a/c   G6 CR.

				£
Jan 21	Purchases PDB/1	690

NOMINAL LEDGER

DR.   Purchases a/c Dept A   P1 CR.

		£
Jan 31	Total PDB/1	240

DR.   Purchases a/c Dept B   P2 CR.

		£
Jan 31	Total PDB/1	460

DR.   Fittings a/c   F1 CR.

		£
Jan 31	Total PDB/1	500

DR.   VAT a/c   V1 CR.

		£
Jan 31	Total PDB/1	180

Notes

Column	Comments
Reference	This is the reference number allocated to each invoice.
Folio	This represents the folio number of the supplier's account in the purchases ledger.
Total	The total of each invoice is recorded in this column, including VAT. This amount is posted to the credit of the supplier's account in the purchases ledger.
Dept A, Dept B, Fittings	These columns are referred to as analysis columns in which are recorded the allocation of the invoice over the various activities of the business excluding VAT. The totals of these columns are posted to the appropriate accounts in the nominal ledger.
VAT	This column is reserved for the VAT included in the invoices and is posted in·total to the debit of the VAT account at the end of each month.

Analysed purchases returns book

Advantages of using analysed purchases returns book (see example below)

Method of recording invoices in analysed purchases returns book

- ☐ Analyse each credit note in accordance with the analysis columns shown in the analysed purchases returns book (see example below).
- ☐ Enter details of each credit note in date order in the analysed purchases returns book recording the amount of each credit note in the total column.
- ☐ Extend the amount of each credit note to the appropriate analysis column as analysed on the credit note.
- ☐ Post the total amount of each credit note to the debit of the supplier's account in the purchases ledger.
- ☐ Post the total of the analysis columns of the analysed purchases returns book to the appropriate accounts in the nominal ledger.

The ruling of an analysed purchases returns book

Date	Details	Ref.	Folio	Total	Tables	Carpets	Chairs	Lamps	VAT
				£		£		£	£
Jan 12	Electrical Supplies	1	PL/E2	115				100	15
30	Rug Company Ltd	2	PL/R1	46		40			6

Date of credit note	Name of supplier	Credit note no.	Supplier's account folio	Credit note total inc. VAT	Analysis columns which will be posted to the appropriate accounts in the nominal ledger ex VAT	Posted to VAT a/c

Illustration

Recording credit notes including VAT in an analysed purchases returns book and posting to the purchases ledger

Assume A. Smith receives the following credit notes:

10 January	CN1	W. Fox sent a credit note amounting to £60 + VAT £9 – allocated to Dept A
14 January	CN2	F. Stone sent a credit note amounting to £40 + VAT £6 – allocated to Dept B

Purchases returns book   Folio PRB 1

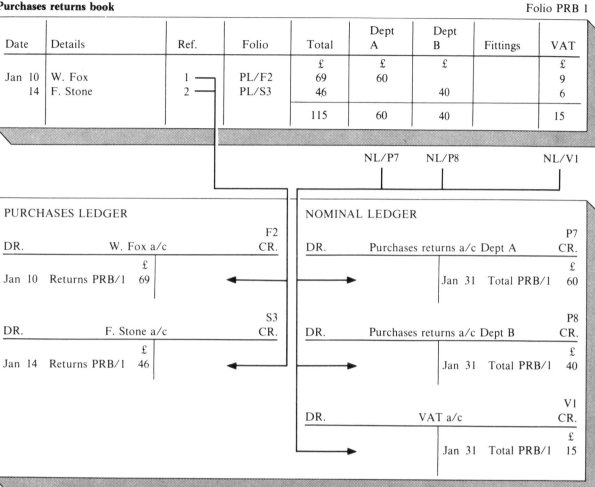

Date	Details	Ref.	Folio	Total	Dept A	Dept B	Fittings	VAT
				£	£	£		£
Jan 10	W. Fox	1 —	PL/F2	69	60			9
14	F. Stone	2 —	PL/S3	46		40		6
				115	60	40		15

NL/P7   NL/P8   NL/V1

PURCHASES LEDGER

DR.   W. Fox a/c   F2 CR.

		£
Jan 10	Returns PRB/1	69

DR.   F. Stone a/c   S3 CR.

		£
Jan 14	Returns PRB/1	46

NOMINAL LEDGER

DR.   Purchases returns a/c Dept A   P7 CR.

			£
	Jan 31	Total PRB/1	60

DR.   Purchases returns a/c Dept B   P8 CR.

			£
	Jan 31	Total PRB/1	40

DR.   VAT a/c   V1 CR.

			£
	Jan 31	Total PRB/1	15

Notes

Column	Comments
Reference	This is the reference number allocated to each credit note.
Folio	This represents the folio number of the supplier's account in the purchases ledger.
Total	The total of each credit note is recorded in this column including VAT. The amount is posted to the debit of the supplier's account in the purchases ledger.
Dept A, Dept B	These columns are referred to as analysis columns in which are recorded the allocation of the credit note over the various activities of the business excluding VAT. The totals of these columns are posted to the appropriate accounts in the nominal ledger.
VAT	This column is reserved for the VAT included in the credit notes and is posted to the VAT account at the end of each month.

Alternative treatment of credit notes

In some businesses a purchases returns book is not kept and the credit notes are entered in the purchases day book in red and deducted from the total of the invoices in that book. The postings to the purchases ledger follow the usual pattern and only the 'net' amounts (invoices *less* credit notes) in the analysis columns are posted to the relevant accounts in the nominal ledger.

Illustration   *Analysed purchases day book used for recording invoices and credit notes*

Date	Details	Ref.	Folio	Total	Tables	Carpets	Chairs	Lamps	VAT
				£	£	£		£	£
Jan 6	Electrical Supplies	1	PL/E2	575				500	75
12	*Electrical Supplies*	*2*	*PL/E2*	*115*				*100*	*15*
20	New Furniture Company	3	PL/N1	5,750	5,000				750
25	Rug Company Limited	4	PL/R1	1,150		1,000			150
30	*Rug Company Limited*	*5*	*PL/R1*	*46*		*40*			*6*
				7,314	5,000	960		400	954

Date of invoice or credit note — Name of supplier — Invoice or credit note number — Supplier's account number — Invoices less credit notes total inc. VAT — Analysis columns which will be posted to the appropriate accounts in the nominal ledger ex VAT — Posted to VAT account

Note: **Lettering reproduced here in italics would appear in red in the actual books**

**How to record
payments to suppliers
in the bank cash book
and purchase ledgers**

The procedure to be adopted when an analysed purchases day book is in use is similar to that explained on page 43. To illustrate this similarity in treatment of accounting entries, assume that W. Fox pays £391 by cheque on 31 January in settlement of his account. The accounts would appear thus:

Bank cash book (credit side)   CB1

Date	Details	Folio	Total	Discount	Purchases Ledger
			£		£
Jan 31	W. Fox	PL/F2	391		391

PURCHASES LEDGER
                                                          F2
DR.   W. Fox a/c   CR.

			£				£
Jan 10	Returns	PRB/1	69	Jan 6	Purchases	PDB/1	460
31	Bank	CB/1	391				
			460				460

How to record refunds from suppliers in the bank cash book

The method to be adopted is to open a purchases ledger column on the debit side of the bank cash book and to post the amounts individually to the credit side of the suppliers' accounts.

To illustrate this treatment of refunds, assume that A. Brown, a supplier to A. Smith, sends a cheque on 10 January amounting to £50, being settlement of a debit balance on Brown's account. The purchases ledger and bank cash book should then appear as follows:

```
PURCHASES LEDGER                                    B3
DR.                    A. Brown a/c                CR.
                          £                          £
Jan 1   Balance          50   Jan 10   Bank    →    50
```

```
Bank cash book (debit side)                        CB1
                                                Purchases
    Date      Details           Folio   Total   ledger
                                          £        £
    Jan 10    A. Brown          PL/B3    50       50
```

Filing procedures for source documents

Document	Filing instructions	Reference
Order form	Date order and sequence	Delivery note Advice note Goods received book Purchases invoice
Advice and delivery notes	Date order	Order form Goods received book Purchases invoice
Invoice	Order of recording in purchases day book	Order form Purchases day book
Credit note	Order of recording in purchases returns book	Documentation used when returning the goods and purchases returns book

Purchases ledger control account

Purpose

To record in total in the control account all amounts entered in detail in the individual accounts in the purchases ledger.

Advantages

☐ It provides, for management purposes, the total amount due to creditors in one account without the necessity of extracting a list of individual balances.

☐ It is possible to ensure the arithmetical accuracy of the information contained in the purchases ledger accounts by comparing the balances on the individual creditors' accounts. If they are not in agreement, this would indicate an error in the purchases ledger accounts or the control account.

☐ Errors can be localised and therefore easier to find and correct.

Points to note

☐ The purchases ledger control account usually does not form part of the double-entry system.

☐ Its main function is to act as an arithmetical proof on the postings from the books of original entry to the accounts in the purchases ledger.

☐ It should be remembered that the control account is merely the total of the individual entries recorded in the ledger accounts and the totals appear on the same side of the control account as they would in the ledger accounts. For example, a refund from a creditor would appear on the credit side of the creditor's account and consequently the total of refunds from creditors will be recorded on the credit side of the control account.

Structure of a purchases ledger control account

Source	Comments	DR. Purchases ledger control a/c	CR.
Purchases ledger	The balance at the start will have been agreed with the individual list of balances extracted from the purchases ledger		Opening balances
Purchases day book	This total will be obtained from the purchases day book which represents the total of the suppliers' invoices		Purchases
Purchases returns book	This total will be obtained from the purchases returns book which is based on the credit notes from suppliers	Purchases returns	
Bank cash book (credit side)	This total will be the amount paid to suppliers and will be obtained from the purchases ledger column in the bank cash book	Bank	
Bank cash book (credit side)	This total will be the amount of discount received from suppliers and will be obtained from the discount column in the bank cash book	Discount	
Bank cash book (debit side)	This total will be the amount of refunds received from suppliers and will be obtained from the purchases ledger column on the debit side of the bank cash book		Bank (refunds)
Purchases ledger	The balance of total creditors outstanding at the end must agree with the total of creditors' balances extracted from the purchases ledger	Closing balances	

Illustration of how the purchases ledger control account is recorded

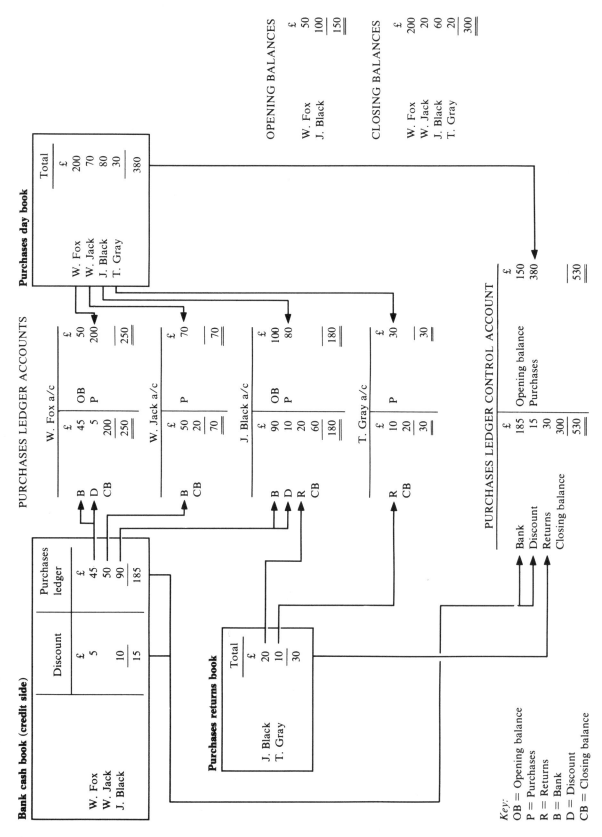

6 How to Control and Record Credit Sales

Method of selling goods on credit

Although each business will develop its own internal method of controlling the selling of goods on credit, some of the main features that should be incorporated in any method used are as follows:

- A stock requisition method should be set up following the receipt of an order.
- An advice note should be sent to the customer giving details of the quantity, type and date of despatch of the goods. No information of the price of the goods should be shown on this document.
- Delivery notes should be sent out with all goods despatched. A copy should be signed by the customer and filed by the business as proof of delivery.
- A record of all goods despatched from the business to customers should be kept and referenced to the delivery notes.
- When the goods have been despatched, an invoice should be prepared and sent. The information included in the invoice is basically the details shown on the delivery and advice notes, including the cost of the goods supplied. Deductions are shown on the invoice for trade discount, if allowed, and, if chargeable, VAT is added at the appropriate rate to the amount shown on the invoice. The invoice, if not pre-numbered in the same sequence as the delivery and advice notes, should be cross-referenced with these documents. A copy of the document is received.
- Prices, extensions and additions of invoices should be checked before invoices are sent to customers.
- When goods are returned by customers they should be examined to verify that the claim is valid. A goods received slip should then be prepared and details of the goods returned and the reason for their return should be shown together with the allowance to be made to the customer.
- A credit note should be sent to the customer advising them of the allowance being made on the returned goods. The information contained in the credit note will be taken from the goods received note. A copy of the credit note should be kept for recording purposes.
- At the end of each month a statement should be sent out to each customer detailing the transactions that have taken place during the month. This information is taken from the customers' accounts in the sales ledger. The statement should be sent out as soon after the month end as possible since many customers delay payment until this document is received.

Control of amounts received from credit customers

Where receipts are issued to customers

- A receipt on an official pre-numbered receipt book should be prepared for each amount received.
- The receipt should show the date, name of customer, amount paid and the discount allowed on the payment.
- The top copy should be sent to the customer and the duplicate retained by the business and referenced to the appropriate cash book entry.

□ The total receipts issued each day should agree with the bank pay-in-slip after taking into account any lodgment for cash sales.

□ All remittances from customers should be checked with the balances shown in the ledger accounts and agreed.

□ Details of amounts received should be recorded in the bank cash book and posted to the customers' accounts.

Where no receipt is issued to customers

□ The amounts received from credit customers should be listed separately and agreed with the bank pay-in-slip before the lodgment takes place.

□ The amounts received from customers should be agreed by two persons before being lodged in the bank to reduce the possibility of fraud.

□ All remittances from customers should be checked with the balances shown in the ledger accounts and agreed.

□ Details of amounts received should be recorded in the bank cash book and posted to the customers' accounts.

Documents used for controlling and recording credit sales

These are discussed under the section dealing with credit purchases (see page 49). The chart of business documents relating to credit sales appears also on page 49.

Accounting method of recording sales invoices and credit notes

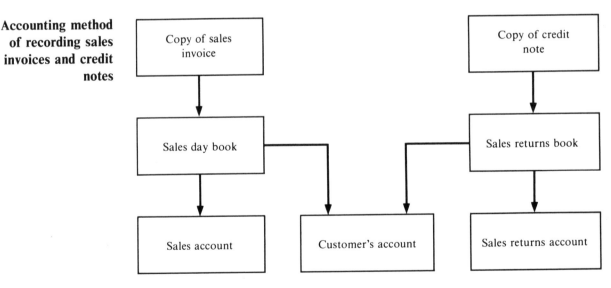

How to record credit sales in the accounts

Sales day book

□ This is a book of original entry which records credit sales transactions only.

□ All credit sales invoices are listed, analysed and summarised in this book.

□ The name of each customer, date of supply of goods or services and the amount to be debited to the customer's account is shown in the sales day book.

□ The total of the sales day book is posted to the sales account assuming that all goods included in the sales day book are for resale. If other credit sales are included such as motor cars, fittings, etc., these are posted to the appropriate accounts in the nominal ledger.

Recording sales invoices in the sales day book and posting to the customers' accounts in the sales ledger

Assume A. Smith has the following credit sales transactions:

4 January   Inv. 1   Sold to B. Clark goods value £500
15 January   Inv. 2   Sold to C. Flax goods value £300
30 January   Inv. 3   Sold to R. Thorn goods value £150

The method to be adopted in writing up the sales day book is as follows:

□ Enter invoices in sales day book in date order and reference them.
□ Post the amount of each invoice to the debit of the customer's account in the sales ledger.
□ Post the total of the sales day book to the sales account in the nominal ledger.

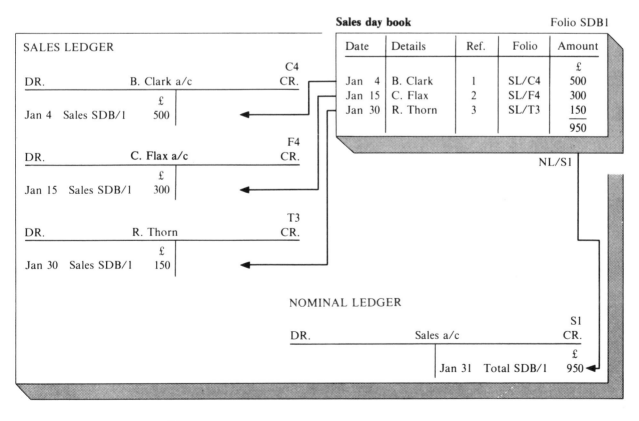

Sales day book   Folio SDB1

Date	Details	Ref.	Folio	Amount
				£
Jan 4	B. Clark	1	SL/C4	500
Jan 15	C. Flax	2	SL/F4	300
Jan 30	R. Thorn	3	SL/T3	150
				950

SALES LEDGER

C4
DR.   B. Clark a/c   CR.
                   £
Jan 4   Sales SDB/1   500

F4
DR.   C. Flax a/c   CR.
                   £
Jan 15 Sales SDB/1   300

T3
DR.   R. Thorn   CR.
                   £
Jan 30 Sales SDB/1   150

NL/S1

NOMINAL LEDGER

S1
DR.   Sales a/c   CR.
                                            £
                   Jan 31 Total SDB/1   950

Sales returns book

□ This is a book of original entry in which are recorded details of credit notes sent to customers.
□ All credit notes are listed, analysed and summarised in this book.
□ The name of each customer, date of credit note and amount thereof to be debited to the customer's account is shown in the sales returns book.
□ The total of the sales returns book is posted to the sales returns account if all goods included in the sales returns book are for resale. If other items not for resale are included then these are posted to the appropriate accounts in the nominal ledger.

Recording credit notes in the sales returns book and postings to the customers' accounts

Assume A. Smith sends the following credit notes to his customers during January:

20 January   CN1   Sent B. Clark a credit note amounting to £20
25 January   CN2   Sent C. Flax a credit note amounting to £15

The method to be adopted in writing up the sales returns book is as follows:

□ Enter credit notes in sales returns book in date order and reference them.
□ Post the amount of each credit note to the credit of the customer's account in the sales ledger.
□ Post the total of the sales returns book to the debit of the sales returns account in the nominal ledger.

Sales returns book   Folio SRB 1

Date	Details	Ref.	Folio	Amount
				£
Jan 20	B. Clark	1	SL/C4	20
25	C. Flax	2	SL/F4	15
				35

SALES LEDGER

C4
DR.   B. Clark a/c   CR.
                                                        £
                        Jan 20   Returns SRB/1   20

F4
DR.   C. Flax a/c   CR.
                                                        £
                        Jan 25   Returns SRB/1   15

NL/S5

NOMINAL LEDGER

                                                 S5
DR.   Sales returns a/c   CR.
                    £
Jan 31   Total SRB/1   35

How to record payments from customers in the bank cash book and sales ledger

The method to be adopted is as follows:

☐ Enter amounts received from customers in the total column of the bank cash book debit side and extend the amount into the 'sales ledger' column.

☐ If discount is allowed to customer, enter the amount of discount in the 'discount' column against the appropriate payment from customer in the bank cash book debit side.

☐ Post the customer's payment and the discount allowed from the bank cash book to the credit side of the customer's account in the sales ledger.

☐ The 'discount allowed' column in the bank cash book is posted to the debit side of the discount account in the nominal ledger.

Recording customers' payments in the bank cash book and posting these to the customers' accounts in the sales ledger

Assume A. Smith receives the following amounts from customers:

25 January   B. Clark paid £460 by cheque; discount allowed to him was £20

28 January   C. Flax paid £285 by cheque

31 January   R. Thorn paid £140 by cheque; discount allowed to him was £10

Using the information included in the previous examples relating to sales and sales returns, the entries in the bank cash book and ledgers would appear thus:

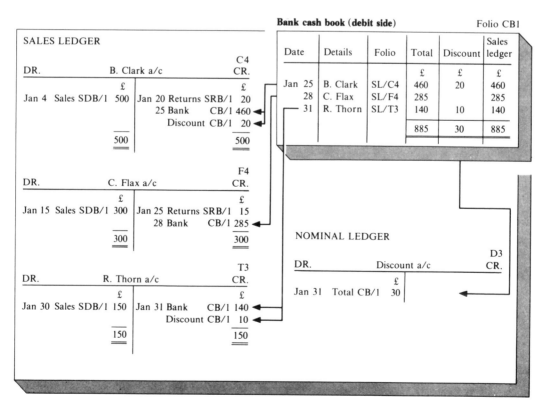

Analysed sales day book

Advantages of using an analysed sales day book

☐ Provides an analysis of sales over departments or other sectional activities of the business.
☐ Assists in the calculation of profit earned in each activity of the business.
☐ Makes it easier to post the analysed amounts to the nominal ledger.

Method of recording invoices in an analysed sales day book

☐ Analyse each invoice in accordance with the analysis columns shown in the analysed sales day book (see example below).
☐ Enter details of each invoice in date order in the analysed sales day book recording the amount of each invoice in the total column.
☐ Extend the amount of each invoice to the appropriate analysis columns as analysed on the invoice.
☐ Post the total amount of each invoice to the credit of the customer's account in the sales ledger.
☐ Post the total of the analysis columns of the analysed sales day book to the appropriate accounts in the nominal ledger.

Ruling of an analysed sales day book

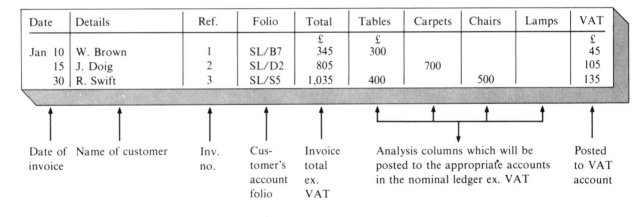

Date	Details	Ref.	Folio	Total	Tables	Carpets	Chairs	Lamps	VAT
				£	£				£
Jan 10	W. Brown	1	SL/B7	345	300				45
15	J. Doig	2	SL/D2	805		700			105
30	R. Swift	3	SL/S5	1,035	400		500		135

Date of invoice   Name of customer   Inv. no.   Customer's account folio   Invoice total ex. VAT   Analysis columns which will be posted to the appropriate accounts in the nominal ledger ex. VAT   Posted to VAT account

Recording invoices including VAT in an analysed sales day book and posting to the sales ledger

Assume A. Smith has the following credit sales transactions:

10 January   Inv. 1   Sold goods to J. Gray amounting to £500 + VAT £75, which were allocated as follows:
To Dept A   £200 + VAT £30
To Dept B   £300 + VAT £45

14 January   Inv. 2   Sold goods to M. Abel amounting to £600 + VAT £90, which were allocated as follows:
To Dept A   £500 + VAT £75
To Dept B   £100 + VAT £15

20 January   Inv. 3   Sold goods to W. Crab amounting to £700 + VAT £105, which were allocated as follows:
Dept A   £300 + VAT £45
Dept B   £400 + VAT £60

Notes to example on page 74

Column	Comments
Reference	This is the reference number allocated to each invoice.
Folio	This represents the folio number of the customer's account in the sales ledger.
Total	The total of each invoice is recorded in this column, including VAT. This amount is posted to the credit of the customer's account in the sales ledger.
Dept A, Dept B	These columns are referred to as analysis columns in which are recorded the allocation of the invoice over the various activities of the business, excluding VAT. The totals of these columns are posted to the appropriate accounts in the nominal ledger.
VAT	This column is reserved for the VAT included in the invoices and is posted in total to the credit of the VAT account at the end of each month.

Sales day book

Folio SDB 1

Date	Details	Ref.	Folio	Total	Dept A	Dept B	Fittings	VAT
				£	£	£		£
Jan 10	J. Gray	1	SL/G5	575	200	300		75
14	M. Abel	2	SL/A6	690	500	100		90
20	W. Crab	3	SL/C3	805	300	400		105
				2,070	1,000	800		270

NL/S1   NL/S2   NL/V1

SALES LEDGER

		G5
DR.	J. Gray a/c	CR.
	£	
Jan 10 Sales SDB/1	575	

		A6
DR.	M. Abel a/c	CR.
	£	
Jan 14 Sales SDB/1	690	

		C3
DR.	W. Crab a/c	CR.
	£	
Jan 20 Sales SDB/1	805	

NOMINAL LEDGER

		S1
DR.	Sales a/c Dept A	CR.
		£
	Jan 31 Total SDB/1	1000

		S2
DR.	Sales a/c Dept B	CR.
		£
	Jan 31 Total SDB/1	800

		V1
DR.	VAT a/c	CR.
		£
	Jan 31 Total SDB/1	270

74

Analysed sales returns book

Advantages of using an analysed sales returns book

See analysed sales day book, page 72.

Method of recording credit notes in an analysed sales returns book

☐ Analyse each credit note in accordance with the analysis columns shown in the analysed sales returns book (see example below).

☐ Enter details of each credit note in date order in the analysed sales returns book, recording the amount of each credit note in the total column.

☐ Extend the amount of each credit note to the appropriate analysis column as analysed on the credit note.

☐ Post the total amount of each credit note to the credit of the customer's account in the sales ledger.

☐ Post the total of the analysis columns of the analysed sales returns book to the appropriate accounts in the nominal ledger.

Ruling of an analysed sales returns book

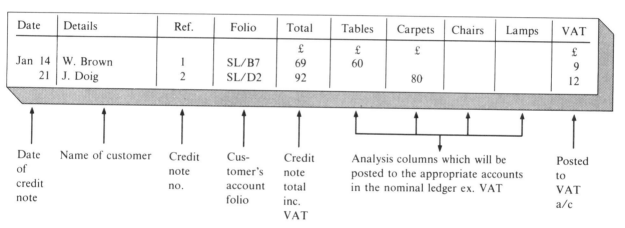

Date	Details	Ref.	Folio	Total	Tables	Carpets	Chairs	Lamps	VAT
				£	£	£			£
Jan 14	W. Brown	1	SL/B7	69	60				9
21	J. Doig	2	SL/D2	92		80			12

Date of credit note | Name of customer | Credit note no. | Customer's account folio | Credit note total inc. VAT | Analysis columns which will be posted to the appropriate accounts in the nominal ledger ex. VAT | Posted to VAT a/c

Recording credit notes in an analysed sales returns book and posting to the sales ledger

Assume A. Smith sends the following credit notes to customers:

15 January CN 1 Sent to J. Gray amounting to £100 + VAT £15 which was allocated to Dept A.

20 January CN 2 Sent to M. Abel amounting to £40 + VAT £6 which was allocated to Dept B.

Sales returns book Folio SRB 1

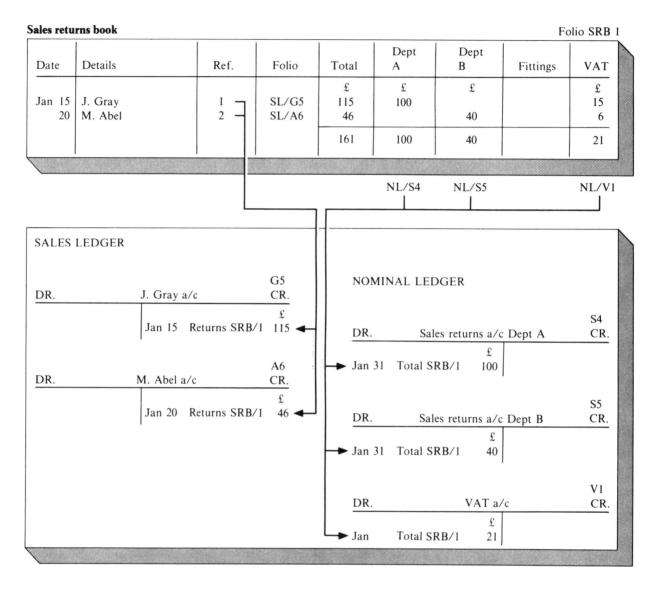

Date	Details	Ref.	Folio	Total	Dept A	Dept B	Fittings	VAT
				£	£	£		£
Jan 15	J. Gray	1	SL/G5	115	100			15
20	M. Abel	2	SL/A6	46		40		6
				161	100	40		21

NL/S4   NL/S5   NL/V1

SALES LEDGER

G5
DR. J. Gray a/c CR.

| | | £ |
| Jan 15 | Returns SRB/1 | 115 |

A6
DR. M. Abel a/c CR.

| | | £ |
| Jan 20 | Returns SRB/1 | 46 |

NOMINAL LEDGER

S4
DR. Sales returns a/c Dept A CR.

| | | £ | |
| Jan 31 | Total SRB/1 | 100 | |

S5
DR. Sales returns a/c Dept B CR.

| | | £ | |
| Jan 31 | Total SRB/1 | 40 | |

V1
DR. VAT a/c CR.

| | | £ | |
| Jan | Total SRB/1 | 21 | |

Notes

Column	Comments
Reference	This is the reference number allocated to each credit note.
Folio	This represents the folio number of the customer's account in the sales ledger.
Total	The total of each credit note is recorded in this column, including VAT. The amount is posted to the debit of the customer's account in the sales ledger.
Dept A, Dept B	These columns are referred to as analysis columns in which are recorded the allocation of the credit note over the various activities of the business, excluding VAT. The totals of these columns are posted to the appropriate accounts in the nominal ledger.
VAT	This column is reserved for the VAT included in the credit note and is posted to the VAT account at the end of each month.

Alternative treatment of credit notes

In some businesses a sales returns book is not kept and the credit notes are entered in the sales day book in red and deducted from the total of the invoices in that book. The postings to the sales ledger follow the usual pattern and only the 'net' amounts (invoices *less* credit notes) in the analysis columns are posted to the relevant accounts in the nominal ledger.

Illustration *An analysed sales day book for recording invoices and credit notes*

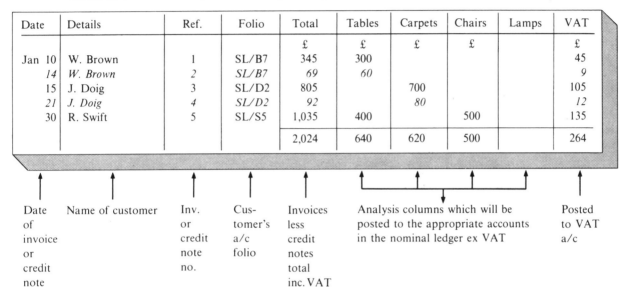

Date	Details	Ref.	Folio	Total	Tables	Carpets	Chairs	Lamps	VAT
				£	£	£	£		£
Jan 10	W. Brown	1	SL/B7	345	300				45
14	*W. Brown*	*2*	*SL/B7*	*69*	*60*				*9*
15	J. Doig	3	SL/D2	805		700			105
21	*J. Doig*	*4*	*SL/D2*	*92*		*80*			*12*
30	R. Swift	5	SL/S5	1,035	400		500		135
				2,024	640	620	500		264

Date of invoice or credit note	Name of customer	Inv. or credit note no.	Customer's a/c folio	Invoices less credit notes total inc. VAT	Analysis columns which will be posted to the appropriate accounts in the nominal ledger ex VAT	Posted to VAT a/c

Note: **Lettering reproduced here in italics would appear in red in the actual books**

How to record payments to customers in the bank cash book and sales ledger

The method to be adopted when an analysed sales day book is in use is similar to that explained on page 40.

To illustrate the similarity in treatment of accounting entries, assume that J. Gray pays £460 by cheque on 31 January in settlement of his account. The accounts would appear thus:

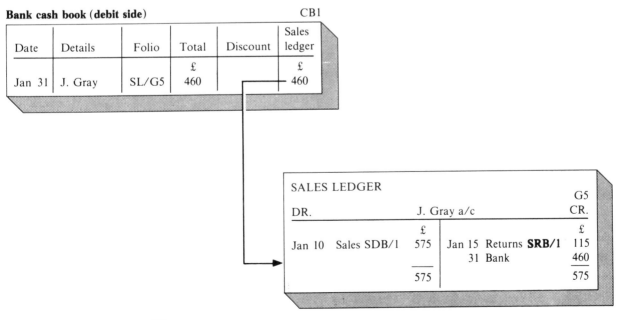

Bank cash book (debit side)   CB1

Date	Details	Folio	Total	Discount	Sales ledger
			£		£
Jan 31	J. Gray	SL/G5	460		460

SALES LEDGER   G5

DR.   J. Gray a/c   CR.

		£			£
Jan 10	Sales SDB/1	575	Jan 15	Returns **SRB/1**	115
			31	Bank	460
		575			575

How to record refunds to customers in the bank cash book

The method to be adopted is to open a sales ledger column on the credit side of the bank cash book and post the amounts individually to the debit side of the customers' accounts.

To illustrate this let us assume that A. Smith sends a cheque on 12 January for £20 to B. Black as a refund in settlement of a credit balance on this customer's account. The accounts would appear thus:

Bank cash book (credit side)   CB1

Date	Details	Folio	Total	Sales ledger
			£	£
Jan 12	B. Black	SL/B5	20	20

SALES LEDGER

                                               B5

DR.   B. Black a/c   CR.

	£		£
Jan 12 Bank	20	Jan 1 Balance	20

Filing procedure for source documents

Document	Filing instructions	References
Order from customer	Date order	Delivery note Advice note Sales invoice
Advice and delivery notes	Date order	Order form Sales invoice
Invoice	Sequence of recording in sales day book which should be date order	Advice note Delivery note Sales day book
Credit note	Order of recording in sales returns book	Documentation authorising credit allowance and goods received book

Sales ledger control account

Purpose

To record in total in the control account all amounts entered in detail in the individual accounts in the sales ledger.

Advantages

☐ It provides, for management purposes, the total amount due from debtors in one account without the necessity of extracting a list of individual balances.

☐ It is possible to ensure the arithmetical accuracy of the information contained in the sales ledger accounts by comparing the balances on the individual debtors' accounts. If they are not in agreement this would indicate an error in the sales ledger accounts or the control account.

☐ Errors can be localised and therefore easier to find and correct.

Points to note

☐ The sales ledger control account usually does not form part of the double-entry system.

☐ Its main function is to act as an arithmetical proof on the postings from the books of original entry to the accounts in the sales ledger.

☐ It should be remembered that the control account is merely the total of the individual entries recorded in the ledger accounts and the totals appear on the same side of the control account as they would appear in the ledger accounts.

Structure of a sales ledger control account

Source	Comments	DR. Sales ledger control account	CR.
Sales ledger	The balance at the start will have been agreed with the individual list of balances extracted from the sales ledger	Opening balances	
Sales day book	This total will be obtained from the sales day book which represents the total of customers' invoices	Sales	
Sales returns book	This total will be obtained from the sales returns book which is based on the credit notes sent to customers		Sales returns
Bank cash book (credit side)	This total will be the amount of refunds made to customers and will be obtained from the sales ledger column on the credit side of the bank cash book	Bank (refunds)	
Dishonoured cheques	The total of dishonoured cheques can be obtained from the journal or from scrutiny of the bank cash book	Dishonoured cheques	
Bank cash book (debit side)	This total will be the amount received from customers and will be obtained from the sales ledger column in the bank cash book		Bank
Bank cash book (debit side)	This total will be the amount of discount allowed to customers and will be obtained from the discount column in the bank cash book		Discount
Bad debts	The total of bad debts will be ascertained by inspection of the journal		Bad debts
Sales ledger	The balance of total debtors outstanding at the end must agree with the total of debtors' balances extracted from the sales ledger		Closing balances

Illustration of how the sales ledger control account is recorded

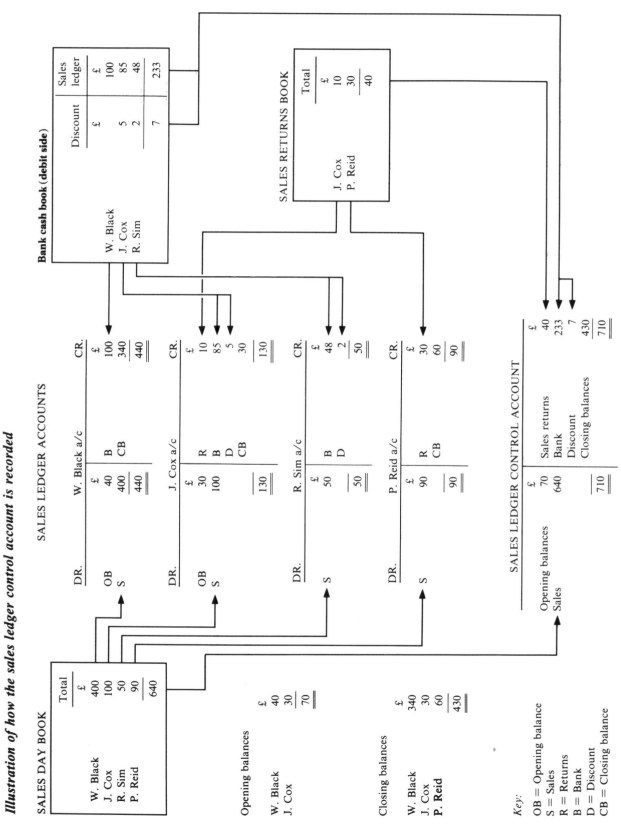

Credit control It is important to ensure that an efficient credit control system is set up where credit sales are involved. Bad debts can arise for the following reasons:

□ Extending too much credit to customers.
□ Weaknesses in debt collection system.

Main points to be incorporated in a credit control system

□ Each customer's account should have a fixed credit limit based on trade or other references.
□ The amount of credit to be extended to each customer should be clearly shown on their ledger account.
□ The credit terms allowed by the business should be made clear to the customer.
□ Constant scrutiny of the customers' accounts should be carried out to ensure that the credit limit or terms have not been exceeded.
□ When a customer does not pay within the credit terms then there should be a clear policy developed for the collection of the outstanding debt.

Debtors' age analysis report

After statements have been sent to customers at the end of each month it is necessary to prepare a debtors' age analysis report so that the credit control system in operation within the business can be closely monitored and the appropriate action to be taken agreed.

Example of debtors' age analysis report

Customer	Total amount owing	Current	1 month overdue	2 months overdue	3 or more months overdue	Action
	£	£	£	£	£	
J. Smith	500	500				—
R. Black	1,000	100	900			Send reminder letter
T. Brown	300			300		Send final warning letter
W. Fox	400				400	Start debt collection proceedings
R. Green	50	50				—
	2,250	650	900	300	400	

7 How to Prepare a Payroll

Purpose

To record the wages paid to employees on the payroll and thereafter post to the appropriate ledger accounts in the nominal ledger.

Main functions of payroll section of a business

- ☐ Maintaining adequate personnel records for employees.
- ☐ Recording time worked by employees.
- ☐ Preparation of payroll.
- ☐ Payment of wages to employees.

Source of information

Example of a payroll

Pay Roll										TOTAL
Week or Month No. / Date		1	9/4							
Details										
Earnings	A	60	—							
	B	10	—							
	C	5	—							
	D									
	E									
	Gross Pay	75	—							
Superannuation										
Gross Pay for Tax Purposes		75	—							
Gross Pay to Date for Tax Purposes		75	—							
Tax Free Pay		24	80							
Taxable Pay to Date		50	20							
Tax Due to Date		17	50							
Tax Refund										
Deductions	Tax	17	50							
	*N.I. Contribution (Employee)	4	31							
	0									
	1									
	2									
	3									
	4									
	5									
	6									
	Total Deductions	21	81							
Net Pay		53	19							
F										
G										
Total Amount Payable		53	19							
N.I. Contribution (Employer)		8	06							
N.I. Total (Employer & Employee)		12	37							
H										
*Contracted-out Contribution included above										
NAME		MILLER K.E.								

Time sheets and time book → (Earnings rows)
Personnel records → Superannuation
Free pay tables (Table A) → Tax Free Pay
Tax tables → Tax Due to Date
Tax tables → Tax Refund
NIC tables → N.I. Contribution (Employee)
NIC tables → N.I. Contribution (Employer)
NIC tables → N.I. Total (Employer & Employee)
Time sheets, time book or staff records → NAME

The above payroll has been illustrated in a vertical form but could be shown with the headings in a horizontal position

PAYE (pay as you earn) The PAYE system of deducting tax from wages applies to all employees, including directors. The tax collected by the employer is then remitted to the Inland Revenue. The employer requires the following basic records to operate a PAYE system:

☐ Deduction working sheets.
☐ Code numbers for employees which reflect the tax allowances to which employees are entitled.
☐ Tax tables which are necessary to determine how much tax should be deducted.
☐ End-of-year returns which give details of total earnings of each employee and deductions made therefrom together with certain other statutory information required by the Revenue on an annual basis.

The tax to be deducted from employees is basically calculated as follows:

☐ The pay due is calculated and added to the total of all previous payments made to the employee from 6 April to date.
☐ By using the employee's code and Free Pay Tables (Tables A), the proportion of the employee's allowances from 6 April up to date is determined and deducted from the total pay to date. The remaining balance is the taxable pay to date.
☐ The tax due to date is calculated by referring to the taxable pay to date in the Taxable Pay Tables (Tables B, C and D).
☐ From the amount of tax due to date, the total tax already paid is submitted, leaving the tax due to be deducted from the employee's pay on the appropriate pay day.
☐ The total of the tax deducted, less any refunds, during an income tax month which is to 5 April must be paid to the Collector of Taxes within fourteen days of the end of that month. A single remittance should be sent covering the tax payment and any National Insurance contributions (see below) which may be due. Details of both payments will be shown in the remittance slip sent with the payment.

NIC (National Insurance contributions) National Insurance contributions are related to employees' earnings and are allocated as follows:

Employee's contribution
(standard rate, not-contracted-out)   8.75%
Employee's contribution
(reduced rate, not-contracted-out)   3.20%
Employer's contribution
(not-contracted-out)   13.7%*

The amount of deduction to be made in respect of the above is to be found in the National Insurance Contribution Tables.

*This figure is likely to change in August 1982.

Recording entries in either payroll or wages book

The method to be adopted is as follows:

Payroll month ending 31 January

No	Name	Basic wage	Bonus/ overtime	Gross pay	Deductions			Net pay	NIC employers
					PAYE	NIC	Total		
		£	£	£	£	£	£	£	£
1	J. Cox	500	50	550	60	43	103	447	75
2	R. Gray	400	40	440	50	34	84	356	60
3	T. Bell	300	20	320	40	25	65	255	44
		1,200	110	1,310	150	102	252	1,058	179

① ② ③ ④ ⑤ ⑥ ⑦ ⑧ ⑨

Column 1   Enter reference number of employee.
Column 2   Enter basic wages from time sheet or time book.
Column 3   Enter bonus or overtime payment from time sheet or time book.
Column 4   Enter gross pay which is total of columns 1 and 2.
Column 5   Enter PAYE deduction calculated from Tax Tables.
Column 6   Enter employee's National Insurance contribution per NIC tables.
Column 7   Enter the total deductions for employee.
Column 8   Enter the net pay for the employee by deducting column 7 from column 4.
Column 9   Enter the employer's National Insurance contribution per NIC tables.

Note that extra columns may be added to show more details of employee's earnings, to show additional deductions from employees, or to show tax-free pay and taxable pay to date as illustrated in the earlier example.

Recording entries in cash book and in nominal ledger

Method to be adopted

Account	Entries	
Wages	*Debit*	Gross wages and employer's NIC
PAYE and NIC	*Debit*	Amount paid to Inland Revenue for PAYE and NIC
	Credit	Employees' deductions for PAYE and NIC plus employer's NIC
Wages payable	*Debit*	Amount paid to employees per bank cash book
	Credit	Amount of net pay due to employees

Example

Using the information in the foregoing example of a payroll, the entries would be made as follows:

DR.	Wages a/c		CR.
	£		
Jan 31 Wages ① 1310			
NIC ② 179			

DR.	PAYE & NIC a/c		CR.
	£		£
Jan 31 Bank ③ 431	Jan 31 PAYE & NIC ④ 252		
	NIC ⑤ 179		
431	431		

DR.	Wages payable a/c		CR.
	£		£
Jan 31 Bank ⑥ 1058	Jan 31 Net wages ⑦ 1058		

Bank cash (credit side)

Date	Details	Folio	Total	Wages	PAYE NIC
			£	£	£
Jan 31	Wages payable ⑧		1,058	1,058	
	Inland Revenue ⑨		431		431

Key to entries in nominal ledger and bank cash book

1 Gross wages per Column 4 of wages book.
2 Employer's NIC per Column 9 of wages book.
3 Payment to the Inland Revenue for the total of PAYE and NIC due for month.
4 PAYE and NIC deductions from employees per Column 7 of wages book.
5 NIC in respect of employers per Column 9 of wages book.
6 Net wages paid to employees per Column 8 of wages book.
7 Net wages due to employees per Column 8 of wages book.
8 Cheque drawn for payment of employees' wages.
9 Cheque paid to Inland Revenue in respect of PAYE and NIC for month of January.

Note   Although the term wages has been used throughout this section of the book similar entries would apply to salaries.

8 How to Deal with Value Added Tax

Purpose   To state the basic principles of value added tax (VAT) and show the accounting entries recorded in the VAT Account.

Introduction of VAT   VAT was introduced in the UK on 1 April 1973 as a new form of taxation. It is charged on taxable supplies of goods and services by a taxable person in the course of any business carried on by him. It is also chargeable on goods imported into the UK.

Taxable person   Any person who is carrying on a business that has a taxable turnover above the limits set out by the government from time to time.

How VAT operates
- VAT is collected at each stage in the process of production and distribution of goods and services by taxable persons.
- The final tax is borne by the consumer.
- Each taxable person supplying goods and services must charge VAT to their customers at the appropriate rate.
- Goods and services supplied are defined as 'Outputs' and the tax charged thereon as 'Output' tax.
- Goods and services received by the customer are considered to be 'Inputs' and the tax thereon is 'Input' tax.
- Customs and Excise send at regular intervals, usually quarterly, a VAT form for completion. This form records the 'Input' and 'Output' tax and the difference therein is either paid to the Customs and Excise or refunded by them.

Rates of VAT
- There are presently two rates of VAT; a standard rate and a zero rate.
- The rate used throughout this book is 15%. This rate may vary in accordance with government policy.
- VAT is charged as a percentage of the value of the supply of goods and services.

Duties of taxable persons
- To record outputs and the VAT thereon.
- To issue tax invoices showing the VAT charge when required.
- To record inputs and the VAT thereon.
- To calculate, for each tax period, the difference between the output tax and the deductible input tax in order to complete the VAT form.
- To keep records and accounts which are adequate for these purposes.
- To keep a VAT account.

Records to be kept by taxable persons
- Records must be kept of all taxable, including zero-rated, goods and services which you supply or receive in the course of your business.
- Records must be kept up-to-date and must be in sufficient detail to allow you to calculate correctly the amount of VAT that you have to

pay or can reclaim from Customs and Excise and enable the necessary tax returns to be completed.

□ Records need not be kept in any prescribed manner but they must be in sufficient detail to enable Customs and Excise Officers to verify them.

Information to be recorded

□ Information must be kept of all activities connected with the business which affect the amount of VAT you have to pay or may reclaim.

□ Information must be recorded of every input of goods and services on which VAT is charged by suppliers.

□ Information on gifts and loans of goods, taxable self-supplies and any goods which are acquired or produced in the course of the business but apply to personal or non-business use.

□ Information on errors in the accounts, amended tax invoices or credits given or received.

Retention of records

□ All records and accounts, including invoices, orders, delivery notes, trading and profit and loss accounts and balance sheets, have to be retained for a period of three years unless the Customs and Excise approve of a shorter period.

Details to be disclosed on the invoice

□ A tax invoice must be issued when a registered person supplies goods or services to another taxable person.

□ Time of supply which is referred to as the tax point.

□ Name, address and VAT registration number.

□ Customer's name and address.

□ Type of supply, e.g. sale, hire, lease, or loan.

□ Description of goods and services supplied.

□ Quantity of goods or extent of service, the rate of tax and the amount payable excluding VAT.

□ Rate of cash discount offered.

□ Total amount payable excluding VAT.

□ Rate of cash discount offered.

□ Total amount of tax chargeable.

Retailers' schemes

□ Special schemes have been introduced by Customs and Excise for retailers whose business consists mainly of supplying goods or services direct to the public without tax invoices.

□ Businessmen are advised to read the booklets describing these schemes to find the one most appropriate to their type of retail business.

87

Example of VAT invoice

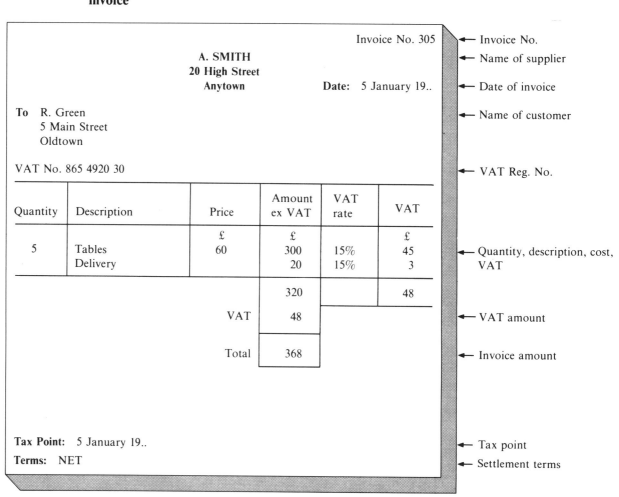

			Invoice No. 305		← Invoice No.
	A. SMITH				← Name of supplier
	20 High Street				
	Anytown		Date: 5 January 19..		← Date of invoice
To R. Green					← Name of customer
5 Main Street					
Oldtown					

VAT No. 865 4920 30   ← VAT Reg. No.

Quantity	Description	Price	Amount ex VAT	VAT rate	VAT	
		£	£		£	
5	Tables	60	300	15%	45	← Quantity, description, cost, VAT
	Delivery		20	15%	3	
			320		48	
		VAT	48			← VAT amount
		Total	368			← Invoice amount

Tax Point: 5 January 19..   ← Tax point

Terms: NET   ← Settlement terms

Note If cash discount is offered then the VAT is calculated on the discounted price.

VAT account   *Summary of information required*

The information required in the VAT account for each tax period is as follows:

1 Output tax (including tax on any goods applied to non-business or personal use) plus tax due not paid on imported or warehoused goods, or services received from abroad

2 Input tax plus tax adjustments affecting amounts due and amounts repayable.

3 The balance on the account will represent the amount for payment or repayment.

Structure of VAT account in the nominal ledger

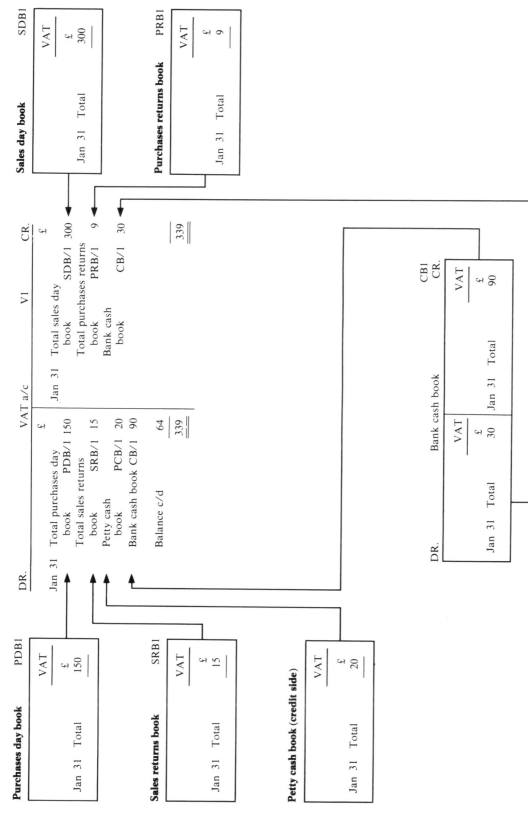

Note 1 Only the total amount of the VAT column in each of the above accounting records has been shown.
Note 2 The balance shown on the VAT account represents the sum due to be paid to Customs and Excise.

9 How to Prepare a Bank Reconciliation Statement

Purpose

The objective of preparing a bank reconciliation statement is to explain the difference between the balance shown in the cash book of the business and that disclosed on the statement received from the bank.

Comparing the cash book with the bank statement

There are two main reasons why the balance shown on the bank statement does not agree with the balance shown in the cash book:

1 Amounts appear in the cash book that have not yet been recorded in the bank statement, for example:
   a Cheques sent to the bank as a lodgment and recorded in the cash book but, owing to the time lag, not recorded in the bank statement until after the balancing date.
   b Cheques recorded on the payments side of the cash book but, owing to the time lag in their presentation for payment, not recorded on the bank statement until after the balancing date.
2 Amounts appear in the bank statement that have not been recorded in the cash book, for example:
   a Payments in respect of standing orders made by the bank but not recorded in the cash book.
   b Amounts in respect of bank interest and charges not yet recorded in the cash book.
   c Interest, dividends or other amounts of income collected by the bank and included in the bank statement but not yet recorded in the cash book.
   d Cheques that have been lodged in the bank account and have been dishonoured when presented for payment. In this instance the bank would debit the customer's account with the amount of the dishonoured cheque and no corresponding entry would appear in the cash book.

Method of checking bank statements with cash book

Step 1 Agree opening balance on bank statement with opening balance on cash book at the start of the period. If the balances are not in agreement, then reconcile them as in the example below.

The following position is revealed in the cash book and bank statement of A. Smith at the start of 19X1:

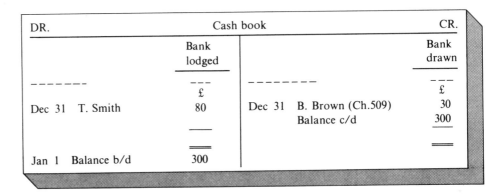

DR.		Cash book		CR.
	Bank lodged			Bank drawn
	£			£
Dec 31 T. Smith	80		Dec 31 B. Brown (Ch.509)	30
			Balance c/d	300
Jan 1 Balance b/d	300			

90

Bank statement for January

Date	Details	Dr.	Cr.	Balance
		£	£	£
Jan 1	Balance			250
3	Lodgment		80	330
4	Cheque (509)	30		300

From the above information, A. Smith wishes to agree the opening balance shown in the cash book with the opening balance shown in the bank reconciliation statement. In order to do this he must check off the two outstanding items in the bank statement, *viz.* lodgment of £80 and cheque payment £30, with his cash book as both items were entered on the bank statement after 31 December but refer to the month ending 31 December. If this is carried out then it will be seen that the starting balance of £300 is now in agreement and he can proceed to check off the other items in his cash book in January with the bank statement.

Step 2 Compare each item on the debit side of the cash book with the credit column of the bank statement.

Step 3 Compare each item on the credit side of the cash book with the debit column of the bank statement.

Step 4 If after comparing the items in the bank statement with the cash book they are found to be in agreement then there is no purpose in preparing a bank reconciliation statement since the balances in the bank statement and the cash book will be in agreement. If the balances do not agree then a reconciliation statement will require to be prepared. The procedure for preparing such a statement is shown in the following section.

Preparing a bank reconciliation statement

To illustrate the procedure to be adopted, consider the following example relating to A. Smith's records for January 19X1:

Dr.   Cash book for January 19X1   CR.

Date		Bank lodged	Date		Bank drawn
		£			£
Jan 1	Balance b/d	300	Jan 4	Wages (Ch. 510)	70 ✓
8	A. Brown	90 ✓	6	A. Black (Ch. 511)	40 ✓
15	T. Green	60 ✓	14	Rates (Ch. 512)	50 ✓
31	W. Gunn	100	31	T. Jack (Ch. 513)	80
				Balance c/d	310
		550			550

Bank statement for January 19X1

Date	Details	Dr.	Cr.	Balance
		£	£	£
Jan 1	Balance			250
3	Lodgment		80*	330
4	Cheque 509	30*		300
5	Cheque 510	70 ✓		230
9	Bank charges	10		220
	Lodgment		90 ✓	310
10	Cheque 511	40 ✓		270
16	Lodgment		60 ✓	330
17	Standing order (AA Sub.)	20		310
19	Dividend from A. Company Ltd		30	340
31	Cheque 512	50		290

Bank reconciliation statement as at 31 January 19X1

	£	£
Balance per cash book		310
Add: Lodgment not entered in cash book		
Dividend from A. Company Ltd		30
		340
Less: Cheque payments not entered in cash book	10	
Bank charges	20	
Standing order (AA sub.)		30
Adjusted cash book balance		310

Note The items which have not been recorded will now require to be entered in the cash book and the balance of £310 shown above will be the cash book balance at 31 January 19X1.

	£
Balance per bank statement	290
Add: Lodgment not yet entered on bank statement	
W. Gunn	100
	390
Less: Cheques drawn but not yet entered in bank statement	
T. Jack	80
Adjusted bank statement balance	310

Note If the opening balances in the cash book or the bank statement had been overdrawn then the adjustments would be reversed, i.e. for *Add* read *Less* and *Less* read *Add*.

Following the steps through as mentioned in the previous section and applying them to this example they would become:

Step 1 Reconciliation of opening balance (see earlier section)

		£
Balance per bank statement		250
Add: Outstanding lodgment		80
		330
Less: Outstanding cheque 509		30
Balance per cash book		300

The above items have been marked thus * in the bank statement.

Step 2 Each item on the debit side of the cash book has been compared with the credit side of the bank statement and ticked thus ✓.

Step 3 Each item on the credit side of the cash book has been compared with the debit side of the bank statement and ticked thus ✓.

Step 4 Since the closing balances in the cash book and bank statement are not in agreement, a bank reconciliation statement has to be prepared. Note the unticked items in the cash book and bank statement are adjusted in the reconciliation statement under the appropriate headings.

Part 3 How to Prepare Your Final Accounts

10 Using a Journal

Purpose	To examine the use of the journal as a book of original entry in a business accounting system.
When to use a journal	If a business transaction is not recorded through a book of original entry then the journal must be used to record the transactions in the first instance.
Uses of the journal	□ To record the opening entries at the commencement of a business. □ To record the purchase or sale of fixed assets on credit which are not recorded through the purchases or sales day books. □ To record any correction of errors which have occurred in the accounting system. □ To record adjustments required for bad debts, depreciation, accrued and prepaid charges, etc. □ To record the closing transfers to the trading, profit and loss accounts at the end of a financial period.

Structure of a journal entry

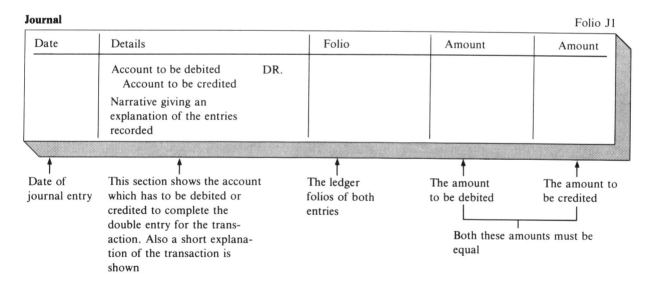

Journal   Folio J1

Date	Details	Folio	Amount	Amount
	Account to be debited DR. Account to be credited Narrative giving an explanation of the entries recorded			

Date of journal entry

This section shows the account which has to be debited or credited to complete the double entry for the transaction. Also a short explanation of the transaction is shown

The ledger folios of both entries

The amount to be debited

The amount to be credited

Both these amounts must be equal

Illustration   *Recording a business transaction in the journal and ledgers*

Assume an item of plant is purchased on credit from Tools Ltd for £100. This transaction would be entered as follows:

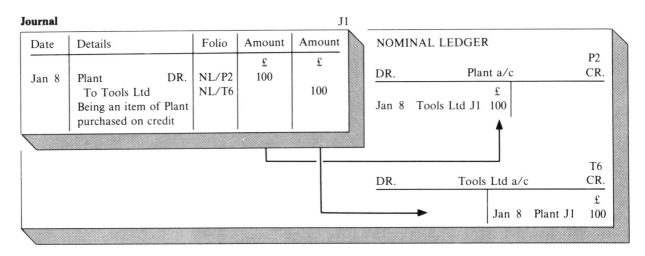

Note in this example that:

□   The Tools Ltd account has been opened in the nominal ledger since the entries have not been recorded through the purchases day book.
□   The account to be credited in the journal entry is written slightly to the right of the account to be debited.

How to use the journal in a business accounting system

Opening entries

At the start of a business the assets and liabilities introduced into the business are recorded in the journal as opening entries before they are posted to their new ledger accounts.

Let us assume that A. Smith starts in business on 10 January by introducing the following assets to the business:

	£
Premises	15,000
Fittings	2,000
Stock of goods	1,000
	18,000

These amounts would require to be recorded in the books by means of a journal entry, as follows:

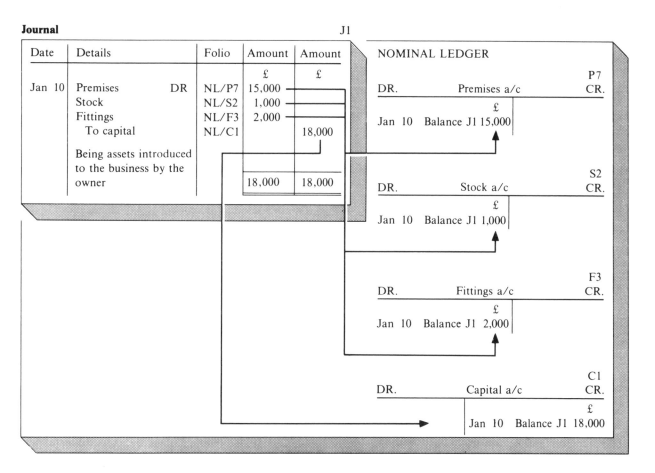

Journal   J1

Date	Details		Folio	Amount	Amount
				£	£
Jan 10	Premises	DR	NL/P7	15,000	
	Stock		NL/S2	1,000	
	Fittings		NL/F3	2,000	
	To capital		NL/C1		18,000
	Being assets introduced to the business by the owner			18,000	18,000

NOMINAL LEDGER

P7
DR.   Premises a/c   CR.
£
Jan 10   Balance J1 15,000

S2
DR.   Stock a/c   CR.
£
Jan 10   Balance J1 1,000

F3
DR.   Fittings a/c   CR.
£
Jan 10   Balance J1 2,000

C1
DR.   Capital a/c   CR.
£
Jan 10   Balance J1 18,000

Note that in this journal entry there are three debit entries recorded and only one credit entry. This procedure is in order since both sides agree in total.

How to record the purchase or sale of a fixed asset on credit

If the purchase or sale of fixed assets is not recorded through the purchases or sales day books then the transactions should be written up in the journal before being posted to the ledger accounts.

Let us assume that on 20 January A. Smith sells fittings for £200 to Suppliers Ltd, who agreed to pay for the fittings in four weeks' time. The fittings were recorded in the books of A. Smith at £300. No entries for this transaction have been made in the sales day book. This transaction will require to be recorded in the journal before being entered into the ledger accounts, as follows:

Journal   J1

Date	Details	Folio	Amount	Amount
			£	£
Jan 20	Suppliers Ltd DR	NL/S5	200	
	To Fittings	NL/F3		200
	Being sale of fittings on credit			
Jan 20	Profit and loss DR.	NL/P1	100	
	To Fittings	NL/F3		100
	Being loss on sale of fittings transferred			

NOMINAL LEDGER

                                                                 S5
DR.   Suppliers Ltd a/c   CR.
                          £
Jan 20 Fittings J1   200

                                                                 F3
DR.   Fittings a/c   CR.
                          £   £
Jan 20 Balance b/d 300 | Jan 20 Suppliers
                       | Ltd   J1 200
                       | Profit &
                       | loss   J1 100
                   300 | 300

                                                                 P1
DR.   Profit and loss a/c   CR.
                          £
Jan 20 Fittings J1   100

Note that the loss on sale of fittings is transferred to the profit and loss account.

Correction of errors

Errors that occur in recording transactions in the business books should be adjusted by means of the journal.

Example 1

A. Smith finds the following error in his books. On 25 January machine repairs costing £50 had been debited to the machinery account in error. This error would be corrected as follows:

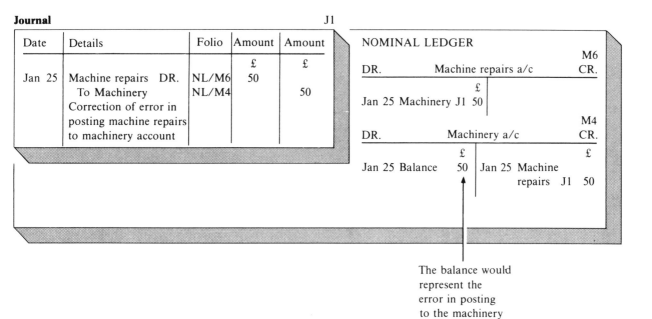

Journal   J1

Date	Details	Folio	Amount £	Amount £
Jan 25	Machine repairs DR. To Machinery Correction of error in posting machine repairs to machinery account	NL/M6 NL/M4	50	50

NOMINAL LEDGER

M6
DR.   Machine repairs a/c   CR.

£
Jan 25 Machinery J1 50

M4
DR.   Machinery a/c   CR.

£	£
Jan 25 Balance 50	Jan 25 Machine repairs J1 50

The balance would
represent the
error in posting
to the machinery
account

Example 2

A. Smith finds the following error after preparing the trial balance. The entries made for payment of £100 by cheque for rates were recorded as:

DR.   Rates   £120
CR.   Bank   £100

An extract from the trial balance revealed the following:

Trial balance

	DR. £	CR. £
Other items	5,910	6,610
Bank	400	
Rates	320	
Suspense account		20
	6,630	6,630

S4
DR.   Suspense account   CR.

£
Balance   20 (difference in trial balance)

Note that the difference in the trial balance of £20 had been transferred to a suspense account and will remain in the latter account until the difference is located and adjusted. The adjustment to correct the error is made, say, on 28 January, in the following manner:

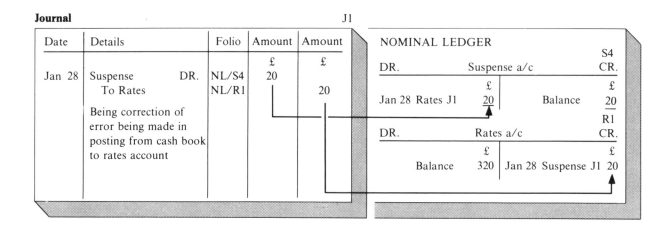

Adjustments to be made during and at end of financial year

A number of adjustments usually have to be made during the year and particularly at the year end to take account of bad debts, depreciation, accrued and prepaid charges, etc. These adjustments are recorded through the journal since they do not appear in any other book of original entry.

Let us assume that A. Smith has a balance in his sales ledger for W. Park amounting to £20. This customer was unable to pay the amount and it was decided on 31 January to write off the debt as bad. This would be done as follows:

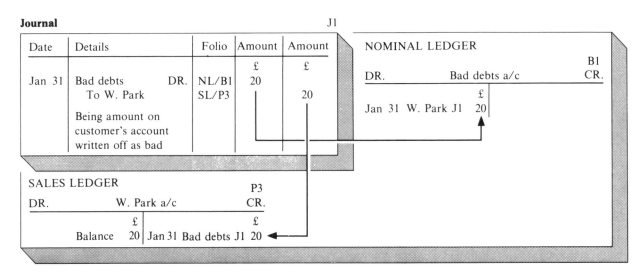

Note that the balance on the bad debts account will be written off to the profit and loss account at the end of the financial year.

Closing entries

These are entries required to transfer the income and expense accounts to the trading and profit and loss accounts and are carried out by journal entries. Below are examples of some closing entries recorded through the journal.

Journal   J1

Date	Details	Folio	Amount	Amount
			£	£
Dec 31	Trading DR. To Purchases Being transfer of purchases at end of year	NL/T1 NL/P1	5,000	 5,000
	Sales DR. To Trading Being transfer of sales at end of year	NL/S1 NL/T1	18,000	 18,000
	Trading DR. To Profit and loss Being gross profit transferred to profit and loss account	NL/T1 NL/P3	13,000	 13,000
	Profit and loss DR. To Wages Rent Rates Electricity Telephone General expenses Being transfer of expense accounts to profit and loss	NL/P3 NL/W6 NL/R3 NL/R5 NL/E6 NL/T5 NL/G6	4,650	 3,000 600 300 400 250 100

Other adjustments to be made by journal entry

Prepaid charges, see page 108.
Accrued charges, see page 109.
Depreciation, see page 111.
Bad debts provision, see page 110.

11 How to Prepare a Trial Balance

Purpose To test the accuracy of entries made in the ledger accounts by listing the balances extracted from these accounts and agreeing them in the form of a trial balance.

Method of extracting a trial balance

- Ensure that all transactions relating to the period prior to the extraction of the trial balance have been fully recorded.
- Balance the bank cash book and transfer the balance brought down to the appropriate column in the trial balance.
- Balance the petty cash book and show the cash balance brought down as a debit entry in the trial balance.
- Calculate the balances on each account in the nominal ledger and transfer each balance to the appropriate column in the trial balance. As there are usually adjustments to be made to the accounts in the nominal ledger after extraction of the trial balance it is advisable to total and balance the accounts in pencil in the first instance and, when the final adjustments have been recorded, balance the accounts in ink.
- Balance all the accounts in the sales and purchases ledgers and transfer the total debtors and creditors amounts to the trial balance. If sales ledger and purchases ledger control accounts are written up, then the balances on these accounts can be transferred to the trial balance since the total of the individual debtors and creditors balances should be in agreement with the balances on the control accounts.
- Add both columns of the trial balance; these should be in agreement.

Simple illustration of a trial balance

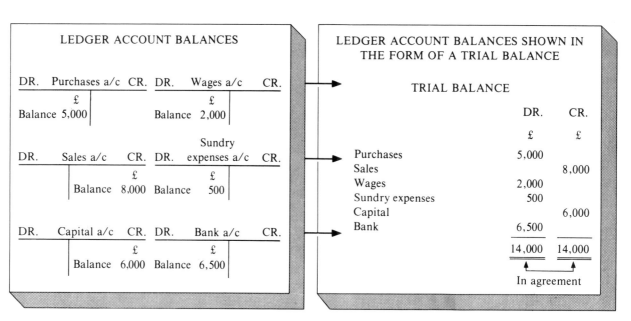

104

Structure of a trial balance

Following the procedure outlined in the previous section, the trial balance should appear thus:

Trial balance as at			
Account	Amount of debit balance	Amount of credit balance	Source of balance
*Bank	X		Bank cash book
Cash in hand	X		Petty cash book
Purchases	X		Nominal ledger
Salaries and wages	X		
Electricity	X		
Rent and rates	X		
Telephone	X		
Discount allowed	X		
Bad debts	X		
Repairs	X		
Sales returns	X		
Sales		X	
Commission received		X	
Discount received		X	
Rent received		X	
Purchases returns		X	
Plant and machinery	X		
Motor vehicles	X		
Fittings	X		
Stock	X		
Goodwill	X		
Buildings	X		
Loan creditors		X	
Capital of owners		X	
Debtors	X		Sales ledger or sales ledger control account
Creditors			Purchases ledger or purchases ledger control account
	X	X	

*If the amount shown in the bank cash book was an overdraft, the balance would be recorded in the credit column.

Errors disclosed by trial balance

□ Arithmetical errors in books of original entry.
□ Balance omitted or miscalculated.
□ Transaction not posted from book of original entry.
□ Amount of debit entry not in agreement with compensating credit entry.
□ Recording of a balance on the incorrect column of the trial balance.
□ Addition error in adding up the trial balance.

105

Method of locating errors revealed by trial balance

- □ Check additions of trial balance columns.
- □ Calculate the difference in the trial balance and transfer it to a suspense account.
- □ Check the calculation and transfer of balances from the cash books and ledgers.
- □ Check that the total of debtors and creditors are correct and in agreement with the sales and purchases ledger control accounts.

If the trial balance is still not in agreement then:

- □ Check that the balances in the opening trial balance are recorded correctly in the books.
- □ Check all additions in the books of original entry.
- □ Check all postings from books of original entry to the ledgers.
- □ When the errors have been located then close the suspense account.

Types of errors not disclosed by trial balance

Errors of omission – where a transaction has been completely omitted.

Errors of principle – where the amount is correctly recorded but has been posted to the incorrect type of account, e.g. a repair to a machine may have been posted to the machinery account instead of repairs to machinery account.

Errors of commission – where an amount is recorded in the wrong account, e.g. sale of goods to R. Cox for £50 has been entered in the account of W. Cox £50.

Errors of original entry – where the incorrect amount is recorded for a transaction, e.g. purchase of goods from Tom Black has been posted as £10 instead of £100.

Compensating errors – where an error in one section of the accounting system is compensated by an error in another, e.g. there may be an undercast in the purchases day book of £10 and also an undercast in the sales day book of £10.

12 How to Make Adjustments for Final Accounts

Stock The following steps are required to incorporate the opening and closing stock amounts in the business books:

- ☐ To record the opening and closing stock amounts in the stock account.
- ☐ To transfer the opening and closing stock amounts to the trading account at the end of each financial period.
- ☐ To enter the closing stock account in the balance sheet at the end of each financial period.

Illustration

Recording the opening and closing stock

Assume A. Smith has the following balances in his books on 31 December:

	£
Opening stock	500
Purchases	3,000
Sales	5,000

His closing stock at 31 December amounted to £700. The books should be entered up as follows:

Stock a/c				Trading a/c				Balance sheet		
	£		£		£		£			
Balance ①	500	Trading ②	500	Purchases ⑤	3,000	Sales ⑤	5,000	Current assets		
				Opening ②		Closing				£
Trading ③	700			stock	500	stock ③	700	Stock ④		700

Key

1 This is the opening stock at the start of the period.
2 This is the transfer of the opening stock to the trading account.
3 This is the recording of the closing stock in the stock account and the transfer to the trading account. The amount of £700 shown as a debit balance on the stock account would then become the opening balance in the next financial period.
4 The entry in the balance sheet is the amount of closing stock in the business at the financial year end.
5 These amounts would be transferred from the purchases and sales accounts in the nominal ledgers.

Prepaid charges An adjustment is required where an expense item has been paid by the business but the amount paid covers a period beyond the end of the financial period. The element of the payment which is in respect of the period after the year end is referred to as a prepaid charge. The following steps are required to record the adjustment for prepaid charges in the business books.

- ☐ To record the amount of the prepaid charge in the expense account.

107

          □   To record the amount of the prepaid charge in the balance sheet at the end of the financial period.

Illustration   *Adjusting for a prepaid charge*

Assume A. Smith pays £500 for insurance on 1 July in respect of a period of twelve months. His financial year ends on 31 December. The adjustment is made in the following manner:

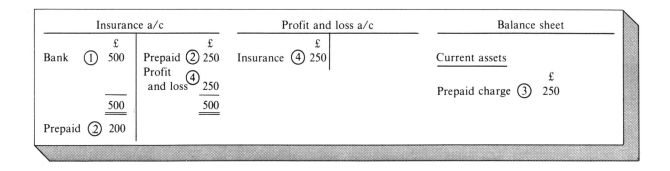

Key

1   This is the amount paid for insurance on 1 July.
2   This is the amount of the prepaid charge representing the period from 1 January to 30 June, *viz.* ½ × £500. The amount is brought down as a balance on the debit side of the account.
3   This entry represents the amount of the prepaid charge which is treated as a current asset at the financial year end.
4   At the end of the year a transfer is made of the net amount on the insurance account, *viz.* amount paid less the prepaid element to profit and loss account.

Accrued charges   An adjustment is required where an expense item is due to be paid for benefits received by the business, but no payment is made during the financial period. In this event the expense account has to be increased by the amount of the expense incurred but as yet not paid or recorded. The amount by which the expense account is increased is referred to as an accrued charge. The following steps are required to record the adjustment for accrued charges in the business books.

          □   To record the amount of the accrued charge in the expense account.
          □   To record the amount of the accrued charge in the balance sheet at the end of the financial period.

Illustration   *Adjusting for an accrued charge*

Assume A. Smith pays £600 in respect of electricity for the period up to 31 October. The amount due, but unpaid, for the period from 1 November to 31 December, the end of his financial year, is £200. The following adjustments should be made:

Electricity a/c				Profit and loss a/c			Balance sheet		
	£		£		£				
Bank ① 600		Profit & loss ④	800	Electricity ④ 800			Current liabilities		
Accrued ② 200									£
							Accrued charge ③		200
	800		800						
		Accrued ② 200							

Key

1   This is the amount paid for electricity for the period ended 31 October.
2   This is the amount of the accrued charge representing the amount due and unpaid from 1 November to 31 December and is brought down as a credit balance on the account.
3   This is the amount of the accrued charge which is treated as a current liability at the financial year end.
4   At the end of the year a transfer is made of the total amount due for electricity, *viz.* amount paid plus the accrued element to the profit and loss account.

Bad debts   An adjustment is required when at any time during a financial period it is decided to write off a debtor's account as bad, i.e. it is considered irrecoverable. The following steps are required to record the adjustment for bad debts in the business books:

☐   To record the amount of the bad debt as an expense item and to write off the appropriate debtor's balance.
☐   To record the transfer of the bad debts account to the profit and loss account.

Illustration   *Adjustment required to write off a bad debt*

Assume A. Smith decides to write off as a bad debt the sum of £50 owed to him by B. Brown. The following entries should be made:

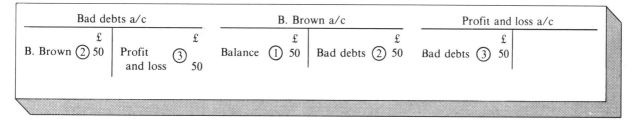

Bad debts a/c				B. Brown a/c			Profit and loss a/c	
	£		£		£		£	£
B. Brown ② 50		Profit and loss ③	50	Balance ① 50		Bad debts ② 50	Bad debts ③ 50	

Key

1   This is the balance on the debtor's account.
2   This is the adjustment to write off the balance on B. Brown's account as a bad debt.
3   This is the transfer of the balance on the bad debts account to the profit and loss account at the end of the financial year.

Bad debts provision

A provision for bad debts is created in many businesses to provide for anticipated bad debts in the future. The methods of calculating the amount of the provision are as follows:

□   Make a list of specific debtors who are unlikely to settle their accounts and then the total of these balances will become the amount of the provision for bad debts.

□   Based on past experience, calculate as a percentage the debtors who are unlikely to settle their accounts and use that as the basis of providing for bad debts, e.g. 2% of debtors' balances.

The following steps are required to record the adjustment for bad debts in the business books:

□   To record the amount of the bad debts provision and transfer it to the profit and loss account.

□   To record the amount of the provision as a deduction from debtors in the balance sheet.

Illustration   *Adjustments required to create a bad debt provision*

Assume A. Smith has debtors amounting to £10,000 on 31 December and he decides to make provision for bad debts of 2% of outstanding balances at the financial year end. This is accomplished in the following manner:

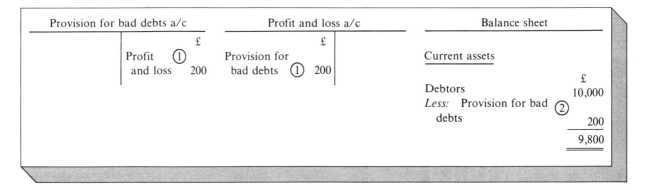

Key

1   This is the adjustment required for creating the provision for bad debts and transferring it to the profit and loss account.
2   This is the provision for bad debts being recorded in the balance sheet as a deduction from the debtor's total.

Point to note All the above adjustments are required to be recorded in the journal before being posted to the various ledgers.

What is depreciation? Depreciation from a financial accounting point of view is simply that an allocation of the cost of an asset based on its service life is charged against the income of the business. This charge is known as depreciation. Depreciation accounting is not a method of asset valuation but a system of apportioning the cost of fixed assets over the operating period.

Causes of depreciation *Physical deterioration from use* Many fixed assets gradually wear out over the years of service as a result of friction, corrosion, rust and the general decay of materials.

Obsolescence This may be caused by new inventions which may come on to the market rendering present equipment obsolete, or improved methods of production require different types of equipment.

Inadequacy This factor arises through business expansion whereby the fixed asset, though still in good working condition and capable of operating for a longer period of time, is incapable of achieving the increased service demanded of it.

Accounting problems The principal accounting problems are:

- Determining the cost of the fixed asset.
- Procedures for allocating the cost of a fixed asset to accounting periods.
- Recording the disposal of fixed assets.

Factors which determine the amount of cost allocation
- Original cost price of the asset.
- Effective life of the asset.
- Residual or scrap value of the asset.
- Method of depreciation to be used.

Classification of assets for depreciation purposes
- Where exact life is known, e.g. leases, patents and copyright.
- Where estimates have to be made, e.g. plant, motor vehicles and buildings.
- Where the asset could last throughout the lifetime of the business, e.g. goodwill, land.

Methods of depreciation The principal ways of computing depreciation are the straight-line method, the reducing balance method and the revaluation method.

Straight-line method

The aim of this method is to write off the cost of the asset evenly over a

111

fixed number of years. The amount of depreciation to be written off under this method is calculated thus:

$$\frac{\text{Cost of asset less residual value}}{\text{Estimated life of the asset in years}} = \text{Annual depreciation charge}$$

For example, if a machine cost £10,000 and is considered to have a useful life of 10 years with a residual value of £1,000, then the depreciation charge would be

$$\frac{£10,000 - £1,000}{10} = £900 \text{ per annum}$$

Advantages of this method

☐ Simple to operate.
☐ Asset is completely written off at the end of a fixed number of years.

Reducing balance method

The aim of this method is to apply a constant percentage to the reducing book value each year so that at the end of the asset's useful life the correct amount of depreciation has been written off. The amount of depreciation to be written off under this method can be calculated by solving the equation:

$$\text{Rate of depreciation} = 100 - 100 \sqrt[n]{\left(\frac{s}{c}\right)}$$

where n is the number of years expected asset life, s the expected scrap value and c the cost of the asset.

For example, if a machine cost £10,000 with a scrap value of £1,000 and a depreciation rate of 20% per annum is to be used then the depreciation charges for the first two years will be:

$$\frac{£9,000}{5} = £1,800 - \text{Year 1.}$$

$$\frac{£9,000 - £1,800}{5} = £1,440 - \text{Year 2.}$$

Advantages of this method

☐ Depreciation charges are high in initial years when most depreciation usually occurs.
☐ Simple to operate when the effective life cannot be accurately determined.
☐ Spreads more even charge to profit and loss account; as depreciation charges fall, repairs and maintenance costs rise.

Revaluation method

This method is used where it is difficult to calculate the cost of an asset in any other way, e.g. loose tools, sundry items of equipment. The amount of depreciation to be written off is calculated thus:

Opening value of asset + Purchases during year less value of asset at end of period (by physical stocktaking).

For example, assume that the book value of loose tools at the start of the year was £2,000. During the year purchases of small tools were made amounting to £500. At the end of the year the stock of loose tools was valued at £1,900. The depreciation charge would be:

£2,000 + £500 – £1,900 = £600.

Advantages of this method

☐ Useful method where there are a large number of small items.
☐ No detailed records are required to be kept for each individual item.

Accounting entries to record depreciation

Straight-line method procedure

a Calculate the depreciation charge for the period.
b This charge is debited to a depreciation account and credited to a provision for depreciation account.
c Transfer the amount shown in the depreciation account to the profit and loss account at the end of each period usually annually.
d In the balance sheet the asset will be shown at cost less the amount of the provision for depreciation on that asset.

Example

A machine cost £10,000 in 19X1. The scrap value was considered to be £1,000. Depreciation has been charged at £900 per annum for the last three years. The current year's charge for depreciation is £900.

Entries should be made as follows:

Ledger

Machine account

		£	
19X1	Bank	10,000	

Provision for depreciation of machine account

				£
	19X1	Depreciation		900
	19X2	Depreciation		900
	19X3	Depreciation		900
	19X4	Depreciation	*(b)*	900
				3,600

Depreciation of machine account

			£					£
19X4	Provision for depreciation	*(b)*	900	19X4	Profit and loss	*(c)*	900

Profit and loss account

			£	
19X4	Depreciation on machine	*(c)*	900	

Balance sheet extract at end of 19X4:

		£	
(d)	Machine — at cost	10,000	
	Less: Provision for depreciation	3,600	6,400

Reducing balance method procedure

This is similar to that described above for the straight-line method.

Example

A machine cost £5,000 in 19X2. The depreciation charge is to be calculated at 20% per annum. The first year's depreciation charge was £1,000. The amount of depreciation to be written off in the second year will be £800.

Entries should be made as follows:

Ledger

```
                              Machine account
                                    £
   19X2      Bank               5,000

              Provision for depreciation on machine account
                                                                    £
                              19X2      Depreciation             1,000
                              19X3      Depreciation      (b)      800
                                                                  1,800

                      Depreciation on machine account
                         £                                            £
   19X3    Provision for            19X3    Profit and
              depreciation  (b)  800            loss       (c)      800

                         Profit and loss account
                         £
   19X3    Depreciation on
              machine     (c)  800
```

Balance sheet extract at end of 19X3:

		£	
(d)	Machine — at cost	5,000	
	Less: Provision for		
	depreciation	1,800	£3,200

115

Revaluation method procedure

a Bring down book value of asset in the appropriate asset account.
b Enter purchases of additional assets in the appropriate asset accounts.
c Enter amount of depreciation charge on the credit of asset account and debit profit and loss account.
d Enter value of asset calculated by a physical stocktaking at the end of the year and credit the asset account with this amount.
e Show the value of the asset in the balance sheet.

Example

The value of loose tools at the start of 19X2 was £500. Purchases of £200 of loose tools were made during the year. The value of this asset at the end of the year was £450.

Entries should be made as follows:

Ledger

Loose tools account

			£				£
19X2	Balance	*(a)*	500	19X2	Profit and loss	*(c)*	250
	Bank	*(c)*	200		Balance	*(d)*	450
			700				700

Profit and loss account

			£
19X2	Depreciation on loose tools	*(c)*	250

Balance sheet extract at end of 19X2:

		£
(e)	Loose tools — at valuation	450

Sale or disposal of assets

Procedure

a Open a disposal account and debit this account with the cost price of the asset and credit this amount to the asset account.
b Debit provision for depreciation account with the total amount of depreciation written off the asset to the date of sale and credit the disposal account with this amount.
c Credit amount received for the sale of the asset to the disposal account and debit cash, bank or debtor's account.
d Debit disposal account with the profit on sale and credit profit and loss account (if a loss reverse the entries).

Example

A machine was purchased by cheque on 1 January 19X3 for £2,000. £500 per annum was written off as depreciation. On 31 December 19X5 the machine was sold for £1,100 and a cheque received on that date. No depreciation had been written off in 19X5.

Entries should be made as follows:

Ledger

			£				£
		Machine account					
19X3	Bank		2,000	19X5	Disposal of machine	*(a)*	2,000

Provision for depreciation on machine account

			£				£
19X5	Disposal of machine	*(b)*	1,000	19X3	Depreciation of machine		500
				19X4	Depreciation of machine		500
			1,000				1,000

Disposal of machine account

			£				£
19X3	Machine	*(a)*	2,000	19X5	Provision for depreciation	*(b)*	1,000
	Profit and loss	*(d)*	100		Bank	*(c)*	1,100
			2,100				2,100

Bank account

			£
19X3	Disposal of machine	*(c)*	1,100

Profit and loss account

					£
		19X5	Profit on sale of machine	*(d)*	100

Point to note When an asset is sold the amount of gain or loss is calculated by comparing the book value of the asset sold with the amount received from the sale. For example, if a machine with a book value of £2,000 was sold for £1,100, the loss on sale would be:

£2,000 – £1,100 = £900

13 How to Prepare Final Accounts of a Sole Trader

Purpose To prepare from the trial balance extracted from the business books, together with end-of-year adjustments, the trading and profit and loss accounts and a balance sheet.

Procedure *Preparing final accounts from the trial balance and making end-of-year adjustments*

- ☐ The trial balance is extended by introducing additional columns to record the year-end adjustments and the amounts to be shown in the trading and profit and loss accounts and the balance sheet.
- ☐ This format enables a check to be kept on all amounts on one sheet and simplifies the production of the final accounts of a business.

Structure of extended trial balance

Account ref.	Details	Trial balance		Ref.	Adjust-ments		Trading account		Profit and loss account		Balance sheet	
		Dr. £	Cr. £		Dr. £	Cr. £	Dr. £	Cr. £	Dr. £	Cr. £	Dr. £	Cr. £
①	②	③		④	⑤		⑥		⑦		⑧	

Key to extended trial balance

1 Folio number of each ledger account.
2 Name of each ledger account.
3 Balance shown on each ledger account.
4 Reference to the year-end adjustment.
5 Adjustment to be made to the amount shown in column 3.
6 Amounts to be shown in the trading account.
7 Amounts to be shown in the profit and loss account.
8 Amounts to be shown in the balance sheet.

Illustration *Preparation of final accounts from a trial balance and year-end adjustments*

The following trial balance was extracted from the books of A. Smith at 31 December:

Trial balance as at 31 December

Account ref.		Dr. £	Cr. £
NL/C3	Capital — A. Smith		25,360
S1	Sales		30,000
P1	Purchases	12,000	
S2	Salaries	10,500	
E5	Electricity	650	
R6	Rates	400	
S5	Stock at start of year	3,200	
M3	Motor expenses	730	
B3	Buildings	12,000	
M2	Motor vehicles	8,800	
F5	Fixtures and fittings	3,000	
List	Debtors	8,300	
List	Creditors		5,900
CB8	Bank	1,600	
PCB7	Cash in hand	80	
		61,260	61,260

The following year-end adjustments have to be included:

1 The closing stock amounted to £4,600.
2 Bad debts amounted to £320.
3 There is a prepayment to be made in respect of rates amounting to £100.
4 An accrual has to be made for electricity amounting to £70.
5 Depreciation has to be provided on motor vehicles at £2,200.
6 Depreciation has to be provided on fixtures and fittings at £300.

From the above information, the trading and profit and loss accounts for the year ended 31 December and a balance sheet as at that date are required to be prepared. This is done in the following manner:

Account Ref.	Details	Trial balance		Ref.	Adjustments		Trading account		Profit and loss account		Balance sheet	
		Dr.	Cr.		Dr.	Cr.	Dr.	Cr.	Dr.	Cr.	Dr.	Cr.
		£	£		£	£	£	£	£	£	£	£
NL/C3	Capital		25,360									25,360
S1	Sales		30,000					30,000				
P1	Purchases	12,000					12,000					
S2	Salaries	10,500							10,500			
E5	Electricity	650		4	70	70			720			70
R6	Rates	400		3	100	100			300		100	
S5	Stock	3,200		1	4,600	4,600	3,200	4,600			4,600	
M3	Motor expenses	730							730			
B3	Buildings	12,000									12,000	
M2	Motor vehicles	8,800		5		2,200					6,600	
F5	Fixtures and fittings	3,000		6		300					2,700	
List	Debtors	8,300		2		320					7,980	
List	Creditors		5,900									5,900
CB8	Bank	1,600									1,600	
PCB7	Cash in hand	80									80	
B8	Bad debts			2	320				320			
D6	Depreciation — motor vehicles			5	2,200				2,200			
D7	Depreciation — fixtures and fittings			6	300				300			
	Gross profit						19,400			19,400		
	Net profit								4,330			4,330
		61,260	61,260		7,590	7,590	34,600	34,600	19,400	19,400	35,660	35,660

Comments on extended trial balance

1 The adjustments column references relate to those shown in the question. Note that there must be two entries for each adjustment, one in the debit column and one in the credit column.
2 The adjustment for the accrual for electricity has been made in the electricity account and extended to the credit column in the balance sheet.
3 The adjustment for the prepayment for rates has been made in the rates account and extended to the debit column in the balance sheet.
4 The gross profit which is the difference between the two columns in the trading account section is transferred to profit and loss account credit column.
5 The net profit which is the difference between the two columns in the profit and loss account section is transferred to the credit column in the balance sheet.

After completing the extended trial balance, the information can be transferred to the formal presentation of the trading and profit and loss account and balance sheet as follows:

A. SMITH
Trading and profit and loss accounts for year ending 31 December

		£	£
SALES			30,000
Less: Cost of sales			
Purchases		12,000	
Add: Opening stock		3,200	
		15,200	
Less: Closing stock		4,600	10,600
GROSS PROFIT			19,400
Less: Salaries		10,500	
Electricity		720	
Rates		300	
Motor expenses		730	
Bad debts		320	
Depreciation — Motor vehicles		2,200	
Furniture and fittings		300	15,070
NET PROFIT			4,330

Balance sheet as at 31 December

	£	£	£
FIXED ASSETS			
Buildings			12,000
Motor vehicles		8,000	
Less: Depreciation		2,200	6,600
Furniture and fittings		3,000	
Less: Depreciation		300	2,700
			21,300
CURRENT ASSETS			
Stock		4,600	
Debtors		7,980	
Prepaid charge — rates		100	
Bank		1,600	
Cash		80	
		14,360	
Less:			
CURRENT LIABILITIES			
Creditors	5,900		
Accrued charge — electricity	70	5,970	8,390
			29,690
REPRESENTED BY:			
CAPITAL — A. Smith			
As at 1 January			25,360
Add: Profit for year			4,330
			29,690

14 How to Prepare Final Accounts of a Partnership

What is a partnership?

Partnership as defined by the Partnership Act of 1890 is the relation which subsists between persons carrying on a business in common with a view of profit. With the exception of accountants, solicitors and stockbrokers, the number of partners is limited to twenty.

Advantages of a partnership

□ Availability of additional capital for expansion of the business.
□ It allows division of responsibility to take place as regards the management and control of the business.
□ The firm can expand more rapidly through specialisation by the partners in the various activities of the business.

Accounting requirements

Where there is no partnership agreement

□ Profits and losses must be shared equally.
□ Capital should be subscribed equally by the partners.
□ Interest on capital is not allowed except where a partner lends the firm money in excess of the capital agreed to be subscribed when there is an entitlement to interest at the rate of 5% per annum.
□ No interest is to be charged on drawings.
□ Salaries to partners are not allowed.
□ The partnership books are to be kept at the place of business and every partner is entitled to inspect and copy any of them.

Requirements which should be included in a partnership agreement

□ The basis of allocating profits and losses among the partners.
□ The capital to be contributed by each partner.
□ The rate of interest, if any, to be allowed on partners' capital.
□ The rate of interest, if any, chargeable on partners' drawings.
□ The salaries to be paid to the partners.

Accounting requirements in partnership accounts

Fixed capital accounts of partners

□ A separate account is opened for each partner.
□ The capital originally subscribed by each partner is recorded in the appropriate partner's account.
□ Any additional fixed capital subscribed is credited to the relevant partner's capital account.
□ Any withdrawals of fixed capital are debited to the relevant partner's capital account.
□ The balances on the fixed capital accounts are shown in the balance sheet of the firm.

Accounting entries

The partner's capital accounts would appear in the impersonal ledger as follows:

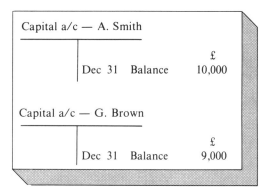

The capital accounts would appear in the balance sheet thus:

Capital accounts	£	£
A. Smith	10,000	
G. Brown	9,000	19,000

Current accounts of partners

- ☐ A current account is opened for each partner.
- ☐ The following matters are included in the current account:
    - *a* Share of profit or loss
    - *b* Interest on capital
    - *c* Partnership salary
    - *d* Interest on drawings
    - *e* Personal drawings of each partner
- ☐ The partners' current account balances are shown in the balance sheet of the firm.

Accounting entries

The partners' current accounts would appear in the impersonal ledger as follows:

```
                          Current a/c — A. Smith
                                    £                                      £
Dec 31  Drawings             7,000     Dec 31  Balance b/d           1,000
        Interest on                            Interest on
        drawings               200             capital                 500
        Balance c/d          2,300             Salary               5,000
                                               Share of profit       3,000

                             9,500                                    9,500


                          Current a/c — G. Brown
                                    £                                      £
Dec 31  Drawings             6,000     Dec 31  Balance b/d             700
        Interest on                            Interest on
        drawings               100             capital                 450
        Balance c/d          2,050             Salary               5,000
                                               Share of profit       2,000

                             8,150                                    8,150
```

The current accounts would appear in the balance sheet thus:

Current accounts		A. Smith			G. Brown	
	£	£	£	£	£	£
Balances at start of year		1,000			700	
Add: Interest on capital		500			450	
Salary		5,000			5,000	
Share of profit		3,000			2,000	
		9,500			8,150	
Less: Drawings	7,000			6,000		
Interest on drawings	200	7,200		100	6,100	
		2,300			2,050	4,350

Profit and loss appropriation account

- ▢ This is an additional account to the trading and profit and loss accounts of a business.
- ▢ The appropriation account shows the following items:
  - *a* Profit and loss brought down from the profit and loss account
  - *b* Interest on capital accounts
  - *c* Interest on partners' drawings
  - *d* Partners' salaries
  - *e* Each partner's share of profits or losses.

Accounting entries

Assuming a profit of £15,650 has been shown in the profit and loss account, the profit and loss appropriation account would appear as follows:

	£	£		£	£
Profit and loss appropriation account					
Interest on capital			Profit for year		15,650
A. Smith	500		Interest on drawings		
G. Brown	450	950	A. Smith	200	
			G. Brown	100	300
Partners' salaries					
A. Smith	5,000				
G. Brown	5,000	10,000			
Share of profits					
A. Smith	3,000				
G. Brown	2,000	5,000			
		15,950			15,950

Note The appropriation account may appear in vertical form as opposed to the two-sided form shown above. An example of the vertical form of presentation is shown in the example at the end of this section.

Interest on capital

- ▢ Usually calculated on the fixed capital of each partner.
- ▢ The rate of interest to be applied is normally contained in the partnership agreement.
- ▢ The amount of interest due to each partner is shown in the appropriation account and thereafter credited to their capital accounts.

Accounting entries

Interest on capital would be treated in the books as follows:

```
┌──────────────────────────────────────────────────────────────────────┐
│               Interest on partner's capital a/c                        │
│                           £                                      £     │
│   Partner's current account ①        Appropriation account ②          │
│   (amount of interest due)   500     (transfer at end of year)  500    │
│                                                                        │
│                        Appropriation a/c                               │
│                           £                                            │
│   Interest on partner's  ②                                            │
│     capital              500                                           │
│                                                                        │
│                       Partner's current a/c                            │
│                                                                  £     │
│                                      Interest on partner's ①          │
│                                        capital                  500    │
└──────────────────────────────────────────────────────────────────────┘
```

Partnership salaries

□ The partnership agreement usually provides for a salary to be paid to one or more partners for work undertaken over and above the normal partnership duties.

□ If partners are in receipt of annual salaries these will be charged in the appropriation account and credited to their current accounts at the end of each financial year.

Accounting entries

Partnership salaries would be shown in the books as follows:

```
┌──────────────────────────────────────────────────────────────────────┐
│                     Partnership salaries a/c                           │
│                           £                                      £     │
│   Partner's current  ①               Appropriation account ②          │
│   account              5,000         account                  5,000    │
│   (amount of partner's               (transfer at end of year)         │
│   salary)                                                              │
│                                                                        │
│                        Appropriation a/c                               │
│                           £                                            │
│   Partnership salaries ②  5,000                                        │
│                                                                        │
│                       Partner's current a/c                            │
│                                                                  £     │
│                                      Partnership salaries ①    5,000    │
└──────────────────────────────────────────────────────────────────────┘
```

Interest on drawings

- Partnership agreements occasionally provide for interest to be charged on partners' drawings.
- The basis of charge is on the amount of sums withdrawn from the business at an agreed rate of interest.
- Interest on drawings due by each partner is shown in the appropriation account and thereafter debited to the partners' current accounts.

Calculation of interest on drawings when financial year ends on 31 December

Date of withdrawal	Amount	Rate	No. of months	Fraction	Interest
	£				£
31 Mar	600	10%	9	9/12	45
30 Jun	600	10%	6	6/12	30
30 Sep	600	10%	3	3/12	15
31 Dec	600	10%	0	—	—
	2,400				90

Accounting entries

Interest on drawings would be shown in the books as follows:

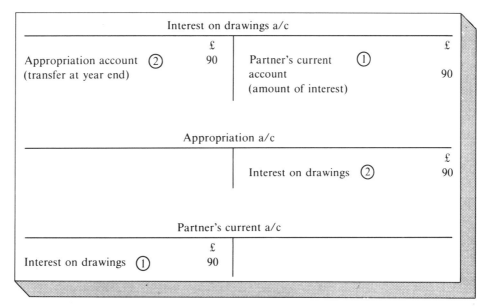

127

Share of profits

- ☐ The ratio of profit sharing is normally provided for in the partnership agreement.
- ☐ If there is no provision in the partnership agreement the profits are shared equally.
- ☐ Profits are shared after allowing for interest on capital, partners' salaries and interest on drawings.
- ☐ The share of profits due to each partner is shown in the appropriation account and credited to their respective current accounts.

Accounting entries

Assuming partner A. Smith received £3,000 as his share of profits then the entries would be recorded in the books as follows:

Appropriation a/c			
	£		
A. Smith current account (share of profits due to A. Smith)	3,000		

A. Smith — current a/c			
			£
		Appropriation (share of profits credited to current account)	3,000

Note If a loss arose then the entries would be reversed.

Drawings

- ☐ Drawings represent the amount withdrawn periodically throughout the year by partners on account of the amounts due to them from the business.
- ☐ The amount of drawings for each partner will be agreed between the partners so that the business does not suffer by excess withdrawals by the partners.
- ☐ Each partner's current account will be debited with the sums withdrawn from the business.

Accounting entries

Partners' drawings will be recorded in the books as follows:

Partner's drawings a/c			
	£		£
Bank (amount of sums withdrawn during the year)	7,000	Partner's current account (transfer to current account at end of year)	7,000

Partner's current a/c			
	£		
Partner's drawings	7,000		

Limited Partnership Act 1907

□ Liability of one or more partners is restricted to the capital introduced.
□ In event of the firm becoming insolvent the creditors cannot claim against the private assets of the limited partners.
□ There must be one or more general partners who are liable for all debts and obligations of the firm in which there are limited partners.
□ Every limited partnership must be registered.

Illustration   *Problem*

Smith and Brown are in partnership. From the partnership agreement is extracted the following information:

Profits and losses are shared equally.
Smith is entitled to a salary of £5,000.
Brown is entitled to a salary of £6,000.
Interest is due on their fixed capital accounts at 10% p.a.
Interest is charged on drawings at the rate of 10% p.a.

The following information is extracted from the financial records of the partnership:

	Smith	Brown
	£	£
Capital accounts – fixed	20,000	15,000
Current accounts	4,000	3,000
Drawings for year	7,000	6,000
Interest on drawings	500	300
Profit for the year to 31 December amounts to £25,000.		

You are required to:

a Prepare a profit and loss appropriation account.
b Show the capital and current accounts of the partners as they would appear in the balance sheet.

Solution

SMITH AND BROWN
Profit and loss appropriation account for year ended 31 December

			£	£	£
Profit for year					25,000
Add:	Interest on drawings —	Smith	500		
		Brown	300		800
					25,800
Less:	Interest on capital	Smith	2,000		
		Brown	1,500	3,500	
	Partners' salaries	Smith	5,000		
		Brown	6,000	11,000	14,500
					11,300
Share of profits		Smith		5,650	
		Brown		5,650	11,300

Note 1 The profit for the year would be brought down from the profit and loss account.

Note 2 The profit and loss appropriation account could also be shown in the two-sided form as illustrated earlier in this section.

The capital account section of the balance sheet will disclose the following:

Balance sheet as at 31 December

Capital accounts		£	£
Smith		20,000	
Brown		15,000	35,000

Current accounts	Smith	Brown	
	£	£	
As at 1 January	4,000	3,000	
Add: Interest on capital	2,000	1,500	
Partners' salaries	5,000	6,000	
Share of profits	5,650	5,650	
	16,650	16,150	
Less: Interest on drawings	500	300	
	16,150	15,850	32,000

15 The Structure of Limited Company Accounts

What is a limited company?

A limited company is a separate legal entity made up of persons who have contributed money or its equivalent and use it for the purpose of earning profit in a business.

Main differences between a partnership and a limited company

Partnership	Limited company
1 Capital for the business is contributed by the partners in agreed amounts.	1 Capital is contributed by the members of the company in the form of shares. Not all shareholders need be directors of the company.
2 The day-to-day management of the partnership is carried out by the partners.	2 The management of the company is carried out by the directors who are accountable to the shareholders.
3 A partnership does not legally require to appoint a secretary to the firm.	3 A company must appoint a company secretary who is an officer of the company.
4 Partners may be paid salaries for their services to the partnership if this is stated in the partnership agreement.	4 Directors are paid for their services to the company. These salaries are approved by the shareholders of the company.
5 The balance of profits is shared among the partners in their profit-sharing ratio as contained in the partnership agreement. If no partnership agreement is in existence this is in accordance with the Partnership Act 1890.	5 The shareholders of the company receive dividends in proportion to the amount of their shareholding in the company. These dividends have to be approved by the company at the AGM.
6 There is no requirement to file annual accounts with the Registrar of Companies.	6 There is a requirement to file an abridged form of annual accounts with the Registrar of Companies.
7 There is no legal requirement to have a partnership agreement although this is advisable.	7 A limited company must prepare a Memorandum and Articles of Association giving details of its objects and regulations governing the rights and duties of directors and members of the company.
8 The taxation due by the partnership is allocated to the partners and paid by them individually. A partnership is not subject to Corporation Tax.	8 Corporation Tax is levied on the profits of the company and payable by it.
9 The number of partners is limited to twenty with certain exceptions.	9 In a private limited company the members must not exceed 50 and be not less than 2. In a public limited company there are no restrictions on the maximum number of shareholders.
10 No legal necessity to have an annual audit carried out but it is advisable that this should be done.	10 There is a statutory obligation on the company to have an audit and an auditor's report.
11 The liability of the partners is unlimited except in the case of a limited partner in a limited partnership.	11 The liability of the members is limited to their capital contributions.
12 A partnership is governed by the Partnership Act 1890 and the Limited Partnership Act 1907.	12 Limited companies are governed by the Companies Acts 1948, 1967, 1976, 1980 and 1981.

131

Differences in accounting treatment of capital in a limited company, partnership and a sole trader

Limited company	*Partnership*			*Sole trader*
SHARE CAPITAL	CAPITAL ACCOUNTS	A.	B.	
£		£	£	CAPITAL ACCOUNT — A. Smith
Authorised				
20,000 Ordinary shares	As at 1 January	5,000	4,000	£
of £1 each 20,000				As at 1 January 8,000
	Add: Profit	6,000	5,000	*Add:* Profit 7,000
Issued	Salary	1,000	2,000	
20,000 Ordinary shares		12,000	11,000	15,000
of £1 each, fully	*Less:*			*Less:* Drawings 8,000
paid 20,000	Drawings	6,000	6,000	7,000
		6,000	5,000	

Note The main difference between the different trading organisations is in the capital structure. In the case of a limited company the capital is subscribed in the form of shares by shareholders while in the other forms of business units it is subscribed as capital contributed by the partners or owner of the business.

Difference in treatment of the profit and loss appropriation account in a limited company and a partnership

Limited company			*Partnership*		
PROFIT AND LOSS APPROPRIATION ACCOUNT			PROFIT AND LOSS APPROPRIATION ACCOUNT		
	£	£		£	£
Profit for year		50,000	*Profit for year*		50,000
Less: Corporation Tax		20,000	*Less:* Interest on capital		
Profit after tax		30,000	A 5,000		
			B 3,000	8,000	
Less: Transfer to general					
reserve	5,000		Partners' salaries		
Dividends paid	6,000	11,000	A 8,000		
			B 7,000	15,000	23,000
Balance carried to balance sheet		19,000			27,000
			Share of profits		
			A	14,000	
			B	13,000	27,000

Note 1 The profit and loss appropriation account is not usually prepared for a sole trader.

Note 2 The above accounts are shown in vertical form but could also be prepared in the two-sided manner.

132

Structure of a profit and loss appropriation account of a limited company

	A. SMITH		
	Profit and loss appropriation account for year ended 31 December		
Ref.		£	£
1	Profit for year brought down		40,000
2	*Less:* Corporation tax		15,000
	PROFIT AFTER TAXATION		25,000
3	*Add:* Unappropriated balance of profits brought forward		3,000
			28,000
4	*Less:* Transfer to general reserve		10,000
	AMOUNT AVAILABLE FOR DIVIDEND		18,000
5	Dividend paid on preference shares of 10p each	1,000	
6	Dividend proposed on Ordinary shares of 20p each	4,000	
			5,000
7	BALANCE CARRIED TO BALANCE SHEET		13,000

Key to profit and loss appropriation account

1 *Profit for year brought down* This is the profit brought down from the profit and loss account whicn is prepared in the usual manner. The remuneration paid to the directors and debenture interest will be charged in the profit and loss account.

2 *Corporation Tax* Assessed on the profits of the company and provision for the amount of tax is made in the appropriation account.

3 *Unappropriated balance of profits brought forward* This is the amount of unappropriated profits brought forward from the previous year. This amount is available for dividend and is added to the balance of profits for the current year.

4 *Transfer to general reserve* Made by the directors of the company as a matter of prudence. It reflects the amount of profit which is retained in the business in a separate reserve fund for expansion purposes.

5 *Preference dividend* This is the amount of dividend paid to the preference shareholders. The tax on the dividends will be paid to the Inland Revenue by the company. The calculation of the dividend paid is as follows:

10,000 Preference shares at 10p each = £1,000

6 *Ordinary dividend* This is the amount of Ordinary dividend proposed to be paid to Ordinary shareholders. This dividend has to be approved by the shareholders at the AGM before payments may be made. The amount of this dividend may vary from year to year, dependent on the level of profits earned. The tax on the dividend will be paid to the Inland Revenue by the company. The calculation of the Ordinary dividend is as follows:

20,000 Ordinary shares at 20p each = £4,000

7 *Balance carried to balance sheet* This represents the balance of un-

133

appropriated profits in the appropriation account which is transferred to the balance sheet and is shown as a revenue reserve. This amount will be introduced into the appropriation account in the following year.

Structure of a balance sheet of a limited company

A. SMITH LTD
Balance sheet as at 31 December

Ref.		£	£	£
1	FIXED ASSETS			
	XXX (Detail)			59,000
2	CURRENT ASSETS			
	XXX (Detail)		35,000	
	Less: CURRENT LIABILITIES			
	XXX (Detail)	7,000		
3	Corporation Tax payable	15,000		
4	Provision for Ordinary dividend	4,000	26,000	9,000
				68,000
	Represented by:			
5	SHARE CAPITAL			
6	*Authorised*			
	10,000 Preference shares of £1 each	10,000		
	30,000 Ordinary shares of £1 each	30,000		
		40,000		
7	*Issued*			
	10,000 Preference shares of £1 each, fully paid		10,000	
	20,000 Ordinary shares of £1 each, fully paid		20,000	30,000
8	RESERVES			
9	Capital reserve		5,000	
10	General reserve		10,000	
11	Profit and loss account		13,000	28,000
	SHAREHOLDERS' INVESTMENT			58,000
12	10% DEBENTURES			10,000
				68,000

Key to balance sheet

1 *Fixed assets* These are recorded in a similar manner as those in a balance sheet of a partnership but are subject to the requirements of the Companies Acts.

2 *Current assets* These are recorded in a similar way as in a balance sheet of a partnership, but again subject to the requirements of the Companies Acts.

3 *Corporation Tax payable* This is the amount due to be paid to the Inland Revenue for Corporation Tax based on the current year's profits.

4   *Provision for Ordinary dividend*   This is included as a current liability since it will not be paid to the Ordinary shareholders until approval is obtained from the members.

5   *Share capital*   The share capital of the company is divided into small amounts called shares which are owned by the shareholders of the company. Shares may be of different denominations, e.g. £1 shares, 50p shares, etc., and also be of different classes. The main types of share capital are:

   a   Preference shares   These shares carry a fixed dividend rate and are given priority to dividend and repayment of capital over the ordinary shareholders.

   b   Ordinary shares   These shares are the most common class of share and are issued by all companies. Ordinary shares carry no special rights and the Ordinary shareholders are only entitled to share in the profits available for dividend after payment of dividends to other classes of shareholders have been made.

6   *Authorised share capital*   This section discloses the authorised share capital of the company which is the maximum amount the company may issue in shares. The authorised capital must be divided into the different classes of shares being issued by the company. The amount is only shown by way of note and is not included in the total column of the balance sheet.

7   *Issued share capital*   This section discloses the amount of share capital which has been issued to shareholders. It is divided between the classes of shares in issue. The nominal value of each class of share and whether they are fully paid or not is shown on the balance sheet under this heading.

8   *Reserves*   A separate section in the balance sheet has to be shown to disclose the reserves held by the company. Reserves may be either capital or revenue and are added to the issued share capital to form the shareholders' investment in the company.

9   *Capital reserve*   A capital reserve is created from surpluses which arise from non-trading sources and are not generally permitted by law to be paid out to the shareholders as dividends. They can, however, be issued to the shareholders as bonus shares. They are usually created from the gain on revaluation of assets or from the premium received on the issue of shares.

10   *General reserve*   This is the amount which has been transferred from the appropriation account and can be regarded as a specific revenue reserve which is being accumulated to meet any future contingencies which may arise in the business. This type of reserve may be paid out by way of dividend if necessary.

11   *Profit and loss account*   This represents the unappropriated balance of profits transferred from the appropriation account at the end of the financial year and is classified as a revenue reserve.

12 *10% Debentures* A debenture is a legal document issued by a company to a person who has lent it money acknowledging the loan. Debenture holders are considered loan creditors of the company and debentures are included in the section of the balance sheet reserved for long-term liabilities. Debenture holders are not shareholders of the company and are paid interest on their holding. Debenture interest appears as a revenue expense in the profit and loss account.

Part 4 How to Analyse and Interpret Your Final Accounts

16 *How to Control Your Stock*

What is stock? Stocks and work-in-progress comprise:

- ☐ Goods held for sale in the ordinary course of business.
- ☐ Raw materials and other items purchased for incorporation into products for sale.
- ☐ Raw materials and components to be used up in the future production of goods or services.
- ☐ Finished goods.

Type of stock *For the retailer or wholesaler*

- ☐ Goods which are in a finished state and available for sale.

For the manufacturer

- ☐ Finished goods available for sale.
- ☐ Partly finished goods which are referred to as work-in-progress.
- ☐ Raw materials to be used in the manufacture of goods.

Other stocks

- ☐ Stationery, fuel and packing materials.

Need for control over stocks
- ☐ To ensure that pilferage, wastage, breakage and spillage are reduced and losses are quickly identified.
- ☐ To ensure that adequate stock levels are maintained.
- ☐ To record information on the value of stocks at a particular time.

Stocktaking This is referred to as the process of counting, listing and valuing unsold goods at the end of an accounting period. The following points should be noted when stocktaking:
- ☐ A physical stock check should be made at the end of an accounting period even when a continuous stock recording system is in operation.
- ☐ Goods should be arranged in a manner which eases counting.
- ☐ Care must be exercised to ensure that proper adjustments are made in respect of goods purchased and sold immediately before or immediately after the accounting date so that goods are not included twice or omitted altogether.
- ☐ All stock sheets should be numbered and the extensions and final additions double checked.

Main types of stock system *Perpetual stock system*

This system provides a detailed analysis of each item of stock on a transaction-by-transaction basis and shown the balance on hand at any time. Each item of stock is recorded on a separate stock card.

139

Example of perpetual stock record card

Description - Chairs

Date	Purchases			Sales			Balance		
	Units	Unit cost	Total cost	Units	Unit cost	Total cost	Units	Unit cost	Total cost
		£	£		£	£		£	£
Mar 1							50	20	1,000
10	10	20	200				60	20	1,200
17				30	20	600	30	20	600

Comments on perpetual stock system

☐ Assists in the control of stock levels and enables re-ordering levels to be easily observed.

☐ Enables total stock valuation to be achieved without physical stocktaking having to be carried out and allows trading accounts to be produced at more frequent intervals.

☐ It is more expensive to operate since detailed records are kept for each item of stock.

Periodic stock system

Under this system an actual physical count of the stock on hand at the end of each financial period is carried out. A list of stock is prepared and against each item is recorded the purchase cost and the amount extended in the end column.

Example of stock list

Stock list as at 31 December

Item	No.	Unit cost	Total
		£	£
Chairs	50	20	1,000
Tables	10	70	700
Desks	5	90	450
		Total stock	10,000

Comments on periodic stock system

☐ It is less costly to operate since few records are required to be kept.

□ Suitable system for small businesses where detailed stock records on a continuous basis are not required.

□ Due to the time taken to carry out the stocktaking it is difficult to prepare monthly or quarterly trading accounts on a regular basis.

□ Difficulties may be incurred in controlling the stock levels when no detailed stock records are kept.

Relationship between stock, purchases, cost of goods sold and sales

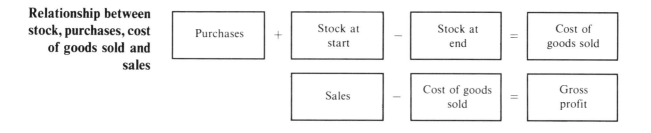

Meaning of some terms used in stock valuation

Cost of purchase   This is the most common method of valuing stock and includes the purchase price of the goods and all the expenditure which has been incurred in the normal course of business of bringing them to a place and a condition where they can be productively used. This would include such costs as import duties, transport and handling costs and any other directly attributable costs, less trade discounts, rebates and subsidies.

Net realisable value   This is the actual or estimated selling price less all expenses of disposal, and, if applicable, any further costs to put the goods into a saleable condition.

Replacement cost   The cost at which a similar item could be purchased or manufactured at the balance sheet date.

Methods used to value stock

First in, first out (FIFO)

The principle used here is that the goods received into stock first are sold first. Thus the unsold goods are those most recently purchased.

Problem

The following information relates to a small retail business in respect of their stock of chairs Type 101:

March 1 Balance of stock   200 units value £1,000
       5 Purchased   150 units at £6 each
       8 Issued   50 units at £5 each
       9 Issued   50 units at £5 each
      10 Issued   20 units at £6 each
      12 Purchased   100 units at £7 each

Record the above information on the appropriate stock card and show the value of the closing stock using the FIFO method.

141

Solution

Description - Chairs type 101

Date	Receipts			Issues			Balance	
	Units	Price	Value	Units	Price	Value	Units	Value
		£	£		£	£		£
Mar 1							200	1,000
5	100	6	600				300	1,600
8				150	5	750	150	850
9				50	5	250	100	600
10				20	6	120	80	480
12	100	7	700				180	1,180

Calculation of closing stock is as follows:

80 units at £6	480
100 units at £7	700
180	£1,180

The cost of goods sold during the period is £1,120 which is the total of the value column in the issues section.

Comments on the FIFO method

□   It is basically a factual method of valuing stock and is used by many businesses.
□   The effect of this method is to value the unsold stock at later prices in the balance sheet and use the earlier prices to calculate the cost of goods sold.

Last in, first out (LIFO)

The principle used here is that the most recently purchased goods are used first. Under this method the cost of goods sold is calculated by reference to the price of the latest purchases.

Problem

The following information relates to a small retail business in respect of their stock of machines Type 200:

March	1	Balance of stock	100 units value £400
	10	Purchased	50 units at £5
	14	Issued	40 units at £5

Record the above information on the appropriate stock card and show the value of the closing stock using the LIFO method.

Solution

Description - Machine type 200

Date	Receipts			Issues			Balance	
	Units	Price	Value	Units	Price	Value	Units	Value
		£	£		£	£		£
Mar 1							100	400
10	50	5	250				150	650
14				40	5	200	110	450

Calculation of closing stock is as follows:

100 units at £4	400
10 units at £5	50
	£450

The cost of goods sold during the period is:

40 units at £5   =   £200

Comments on the LIFO method

□ This method assumes that the initial purchase of goods is regarded as the base stock which should remain intact throughout the lifetime of the business.

□ If this method is used, the earlier prices are used for valuing unsold stocks for balance sheet purposes and the current prices to calculate the cost of goods sold for the trading account.

Average cost

The calculation of stock under this method is made on the basis of the application to the units of stock on hand of an average price computed by dividing the total cost of units by the total number of such units. This average price may be arrived at by means of a continuous calculation, a periodic calculation or a moving periodic calculation.

Problem

The following information relates to a small manufacturing business in respect of their stock of machine parts Type 300:

March 1	Balance of stock	40 units value £1,600
7	Purchased	60 units value £3,000
10	Issued	30 units at average cost price

Record the above information on the appropriate stock card.

143

Solution

Description - Machine parts type 300

Date	Detail	Units	Value	Average cost
			£	£
Mar 1	Balance	40	1,600	40
7	Purchases	60	3,000	50
		100	4,600	46
10	Issued	30	1,380	46
		70	3,220	46

Comments on average cost method:

□ This method attempts to consolidate the different prices paid for stock over a period of time.

□ The difficulty of applying this method arises in the number of calculations which are required to determine the unit price of each item where cost of purchases vary considerably.

Retail inventory method

This method is based on the principle that if the amount of sales of a business is known, an estimate of the closing stock and cost of goods sold for the period may be made. This is based on the fact that it is always possible to calculate the relationship between cost price and selling price when the percentage mark-up on cost is known.

How to apply the mark-up

Assume that goods are purchased for £1,000 and it is decided that a mark-up of 50% is added to the cost of the goods. Then the

Cost price of the goods will be	£1,000
Selling price will be (£1,000 + 50%)	= £1,500
Gross profit will be (£1,500 – £1,000)	= £500

It is important to note that although the mark-up is 50% on purchases the gross profit margin on sales is only $33\frac{1}{3}\%$.

The calculation of gross profit margin is as follows:

$$\frac{\text{Gross profit}}{\text{Selling price}} \times 100 = \frac{500}{1,500} \times 100 = 33\frac{1}{3}\%$$

Using the same figures it can be seen that the relationship of cost of goods sold to sales is $66\frac{2}{3}\%$. The calculation is:

$$\frac{\text{Cost of goods}}{\text{Selling price}} \times 100 = \frac{1,000}{1,500} \times 100 = 66\frac{2}{3}\%$$

144

From the foregoing it can be concluded that if a mark-up of 50% is made on purchases of goods then:

Gross profit will be $33\frac{1}{3}$% of sales
Cost of goods sold will be $66\frac{2}{3}$% of sales

Comparison of mark-up on purchases with gross profit percentage and cost of goods sold

Mark-up, %	Gross profit percentage on sales	Cost of goods sold as a percentage of sales
25	20	80
$33\frac{1}{3}$	25	75
50	$33\frac{1}{3}$	$66\frac{2}{3}$
100	50	50

Problem

The following example illustrates the technique of calculating the estimated closing stock figure and the cost of goods sold for the month of March given the following information obtained from the records of a small retail shop:

Stock at 1 March at cost	£6,000
Purchases at cost	£5,000
Sales	£8,750

A mark-up of 25% was added to the cost price of goods.

Solution

Conversion of cost price of goods to selling price

	Cost, £	Selling price, £
Stock at 1 March	6,000	7,500
Purchases	5,000	6,250
	11,000	13,750

Calculation of cost of goods sold

$$\frac{\text{Cost of goods}}{\text{Selling price}} \times \text{Sales} = \frac{11,000}{13,750} \times 8,750 = \text{£7,000}$$

Calculation of closing stock

Cost of goods less cost of goods sold = 11,000 – 7,000 = £4,000

The above calculations can be proved by preparing a trading account for March:

Trading account for March

		£	£
Sales			8,750
Less: Cost of goods sold			
Opening stock		6,000	
Add: Purchases		5,000	
		11,000	
Less: Closing stock		4,000	7,000
Gross profit			1,750

If the gross profit is £1,750 on a mark-up of 25% on cost then the gross profit should be 20%, i.e.

$$\frac{\text{Gross profit}}{\text{Sales}} \times 100$$

$$= \frac{1,750}{8,750} \times 100 = 20\%$$

Comments on retail inventory method

☐ Can be used when retail businesses find it difficult to maintain stock records as outlined in the methods described earlier and yet wish to prepare financial trading statements at say monthly intervals.

☐ As the mark-up is usually a set percentage added to the purchase price of the goods, it is simple to calculate the closing stock figure and the cost of goods sold.

☐ Any reduction or increases in the selling price of goods can be recorded separately and adjusted on the selling price.

☐ Where there are several mark-ups used in a business, this method can still be used to advantage. Goods bought and sold are recorded under the appropriate mark-up and separate trading accounts prepared for each mark-up group. The gross profits of all the groups will become the gross profit of the business as a whole.

17 How to Interpret the Annual Accounts of Your Business

Purpose To analyse and interpret the trading, profit and loss accounts and balance sheet of a business.

The need to interpret financial statements

- ☐ To ascertain if the level of profits earned justifies the continuance of the business.
- ☐ To establish whether the business is able to meet its debts in the short and long term.
- ☐ To discover if sales have increased over the years.
- ☐ To determine the most profitable and least profitable activities of the business.
- ☐ To ascertain if profits are being maximised.
- ☐ To ensure that the costs in the profit and loss account are being controlled.
- ☐ To ensure that stocks are being maintained at an adequate level.
- ☐ To establish trends, changes and relationships in the amounts disclosed in the annual accounts.

Basic techniques used in analysing annual accounts

Ratio analysis

- ☐ This technique involves the calculation of financial ratios from information disclosed in the financial accounts.
- ☐ The financial ratios are useful in forecasting and planning for the future.
- ☐ The ratios can be used for comparison with results achieved in other businesses in the same industry.

Trend analysis

- ☐ This technique can be used to assist in the assessment of the financial stability of a business.
- ☐ Comparisons may be made between different accounting periods, different businesses in the same trade and industry, and actual results and budgeted results to determine if the actual performance has fallen short or exceeded expected performance.
- ☐ It is essential when using this technique that the data being compared are defined in the same terms and measured on a similar and consistent basis.

Points to be considered by a businessman in the use of ratio analysis

- ☐ Meaningless ratios should be avoided.
- ☐ Ratios which may be misinterpreted by management should be discarded.
- ☐ Some ratios can only be of value when compared with other businesses of a similar type and size.
- ☐ Adjustments may have to be made for inflation before calculating some ratios particularly where trend analysis is being used.

147

□ It must be remembered that ratio analysis is a useful aid for reaching correct business decisions but it never replaces sound business judgment.

Analysing the trading account

Important points to examine:

□ Trend of sales.
□ Gross profit percentage.
□ Rate of stock turnover.

Ratio	Basis of calculation	Purpose
Gross profit percentage	$\dfrac{\text{Gross profit}}{\text{Sales}} \times 100$	To calculate the profit margin earned on sales
Rate of stock turnover	$\dfrac{\text{Cost of goods sold}}{\text{Stock}}$	To calculate the number of times stock is being turned over in a given period of time

Analysing the profit and loss account

Important points to examine:

□ Expenses compared to sales.
□ Net profit as a percentage of sales.
□ Trend of expenses.

Ratio	Basis of calculation	Purpose
Expenses to sales	$\dfrac{\text{Expense}}{\text{Sales}} \times 100$	To calculate the proportion of sales income absorbed by revenue expenses
Net profit to sales	$\dfrac{\text{Net profit}}{\text{Sales}} \times 100$	To calculate the overall profit as a percentage of sales

Analysing the balance sheet

Important points to examine:

- ☐ The return on capital invested in the business.
- ☐ The ability of a business to meet its debts.
- ☐ The amount of credit being taken by the customers of the business.

Ratio	Basis of calculation	Purpose
Working capital or current ratio	$\dfrac{\text{Current assets}}{\text{Current liabilities}}$	To determine if the business is able to meet its debts out of current assets
Liquidity ratio	$\dfrac{\text{Current assets less stock}}{\text{Current liabilities}}$	To determine if the business can meet its debts out of liquid assets (current assets less stock)
Debtors to sales ratio	$\dfrac{\text{Debtors}}{\text{Credit sales}} \times 12$	To find out the average credit taken by customers
Return on capital invested	*Sole trader:* $\dfrac{\text{Profit}}{\text{Capital}} \times 100$ *Partnership:* $\dfrac{\text{Partnership profit}}{\text{Total capital accounts}} \times 100$ *Company:* $\dfrac{\text{Profit before tax}}{\text{Capital employed}} \times 100$	To find out the return on the capital invested compared with the profit earned

Important points to consider when interpreting annual accounts

- ☐ Reduce the number of figures, wherever possible, by grouping similar items, e.g. administration expenses, selling expenses.
- ☐ Look for significant relationships between the items, e.g. debtors to sales.
- ☐ Simplify the relationships by expressing them as ratios, e.g. gross profit percentage.
- ☐ Compare items and ratios with some kind of standard or yardstick, e.g. previous years' figures or comparative ratios of other businesses in the same trade or industry.

Illustration *Method of interpreting the annual accounts of a business*

The following are the annual accounts of the financial results of A. Smith for three years ending on 31 December:

Trading and profit and loss accounts

	£	Year 1 £	£	Year 2 £	£	Year 3 £
Sales		78,000		93,000		117,000
Less: Cost of goods sold		52,000		70,000		93,000
Gross profit		26,000		23,000		24,000
Less: Selling expenses	10,000		10,000		11,000	
Administration expenses	8,000	18,000	8,000	18,000	9,000	20,000
Net profit		8,000		5,000		4,000

Balance sheet as at 31 December

	£	Year 1 £	£	Year 2 £	£	Year 3 £
FIXED ASSETS						
Plant and motor vehicles	18,000		25,000		25,000	
Less: Depreciation	7,000	11,000	8,000	17,000	11,000	14,000
CURRENT ASSETS						
Stock	13,000		20,800		26,000	
Debtors	10,400	23,400	15,600	36,400	20,800	46,800
		34,400		53,400		60,800
CAPITAL ACCOUNT		25,300		28,200		38,200
CURRENT LIABILITIES						
Creditors	7,800		7,800		13,000	
Bank	1,300	9,100	17,400	25,200	9,600	22,600
		34,400		53,400		60,800

Note A. Smith introduced £8,000 of additional capital into the business in Year 3.

Procedure to be adopted in analysing the annual accounts

Trading account ratio and trends:
1 Trend analysis of sales.
2 Gross profit percentage.
3 Rate of stock turnover.

Profit and loss account ratios:
1 Expense to sales ratio for all expenses.
2 Net profit to sales.

Balance sheet ratios:
1 Working capital or current ratio.
2 Liquidity ratio.

3 Debtors to sales ratio.
4 Return on capital invested ratio.

Note Other appropriate ratios may be calculated if considered relevant, e.g. sales to fixed assets.

☐ Brief comments should be shown against the calculation of each ratio for management control purposes.
☐ A short summary on the profitability and liquidity of the business should be prepared.

Analysis of trading account

	Year 1	Year 2	Year 3	Comment
Sales trend, %	100	119	150	Gradual increase
Gross profit percentage, %	33	25	20	Decreasing and unsatisfactory. Further investigation required
Rate of stock turnover, times	4	3.4	3.6	Reasonably stable but must be compared with expected turnover in similar trade or industry

Note Basis of calculation of sales trend

	Year 1	Year 2	Year 3
Sales trend	78,000	$\dfrac{93,000}{78,000} \times 100$	$\dfrac{117,000}{78,000} \times 100$
	= 100%	= 119%	= 150%

Analysis of profit and loss account

	Year 1	Year 2	Year 3	Comment
Expenses to sales:				
Selling, %	12.8	10.8	9.4	Gradual improvement
Administration, %	10.3	8.6	7.7	Gradual improvement
Net profit to sales, %	10.3	5.4	3.4	Substantial fall caused by drop in gross profit

Analysis of balance sheet

	Year 1	Year 2	Year 3	Comment
Working capital or current ratio	2.6:1	1.4:1	2.1:1	Erratic, low level in Year 2 but improved in Year 3
Liquidity ratio	1.1:1	0.6:1	0.9:1	Erratic and gradually decreasing in Year 3 due to high levels of stock
Debtors to sales, months	1.6	2.0	2.1	Gradual increase in credit taken by customers. Credit control system required to be improved
Return on capital invested, %	3.2	1.8	1.6	Inadequate return on capital invested in Year 3. Action must be taken to improve profitability

Note The techniques used to solve this problem can apply to a sole trader, a partnership, or a limited company.

General comments on the profitability and liquidity of the business

Profitability

Gross profit The rate of gross profit has reduced substantially each year although sales have increased over the period by 50%.

Expenses The expenses have increased slightly over the three years, but have shown a reduction when compared as a percentage of sales.

Net profit The net profit of the business is totally inadequate. This has been caused by the serious decline in the rate of gross profit. Unless the position is improved the business will quickly run into a loss situation.

Return on capital invested The return shown on capital invested for Year 3 is inadequate. The owner of the business should expect the return to be substantially in excess of that shown otherwise it is pointless remaining in business.

Liquidity

From the following table it can be seen that the working capital was reduced substantially in Year 2 but, due to the introduction of £8,000 capital in Year 3, this position has improved. If this capital had not been introduced the business would have been in serious financial difficulties. One of the problems in the business is obviously a weakness in the debt collection system since customers are taking considerably longer to pay their accounts. Stricter control over debt collection would improve the cash position.

	Year 1	Year 2	Year 3
	£	£	£
Current assets	23,400	36,400	46,800
Current liabilities	9,100	25,200	22,600
Working capital	14,300	11,200	24,200

Checklist of factors that may affect the gross profit margin of a business

☐ Errors in physical stocktaking at year end.

☐ Invoices omitted from books but amount of goods received included in stock list.

☐ Changes in mark-downs and allowances on goods.

☐ Errors in charging out goods to customers.

☐ Returns from customers not recorded.

☐ Increase or decrease in selling price without any corresponding increase in purchase costs.

☐ Increase in purchase costs without a corresponding increase in selling price of goods sold.

☐ Cash from sales or goods misappropriated.

☐ Losses through waste or deterioration.

☐ Changes in sales mix where all goods sold do not have same profit margin.

The problem of overtrading

☐ This arises when a business is attempting to do too much on too little capital.

☐ It is usually due to an increase in sales causing the amount due by customers to rise. This in turn means more stock to be carried to meet the customers' demands.

☐ When overtrading occurs it is found that there is a worsening liquid position which is evidenced by a fall in the liquidity ratio accompanied by an increase in stock and debtors.

☐ The only solution to the problem is usually an increase in overdraft facilities from the bank and, in the longer term, a new injection of capital.

Further points

Other matters that should be examined when assessing the financial stability of a business particularly when it is being purchased on the basis of the annual accounts

☐ Has the business made proper provision in the accounts for
Bad debts
Depreciation on fixed assets
Taxation (in the case of a limited company)
Any other contingencies?

153

- □ Are there any undisclosed liabilities or contingent liabilities such as lawsuits on patents or other infringements?
- □ Are any commitments for capital expenditure not included in the accounts?
- □ Does the company have the necessary funds to replace and purchase any required fixed assets?
- □ Is the business being subject to an investigation by the Inland Revenue or Customs and Excise over tax matters?
- □ Do the amounts in the annual accounts relating to fixed and current assets reflect a fair value of them?

18 Cash Forecasting and Budgeting

What is a cash forecast?

A cash forecast or budget is a financial statement that reveals estimated future cash position of a business by listing the estimated future cash receipts and deducting the estimated future cash payments.

Necessity for preparing a cash forecast

- ☐ To ensure that a business is able to meet its financial commitments as they fall due.
- ☐ To minimise the charge for bank interest by ensuring that borrowing requirements are kept to a minimum.
- ☐ To assist in determining policies for the purchase of fixed assets and the financing of other activities of the business.
- ☐ The preparation of the forecast requires a review of the present position and future plans, thus increasing the efficiency of the business.
- ☐ Greatly assists the control of cash in businesses which are seasonal in nature when large amounts of cash are required in one part of a year and there is an excess of cash at another part.
- ☐ To provide funds for taxation payments.

Types of cash forecasts

There are two main types of cash forecast:

1 *Short-term forecast* To determine the cash requirements for short-term operations and usually prepared on a monthly basis.
2 *Long-term forecast* To determine the cash requirements for proposed long-term plans for capital projects and possibly prepared for a full year period.

Illustration

Three-month cash forecast – basic layout

	January	February	March
Estimated receipts			
Cash sales			
Cash received from debtors			
Rent from property			
Bank interest received			
Additional capital paid in by owner			
Total estimated receipts			
Estimated payments			
Wages			
Cash purchases			
Cash paid to creditors			
Other expenses:			
Taxation			
Purchase of plant			
Total estimated payments			
Cash/bank balance at start of month			
Excess of receipts over payment (net inflow)			
Excess of payments over receipts (net outflow)			
Cash/bank balance end of month			

Completed three-month cash forecast

A. Smith provides the following information which has been extracted from his financial records and also from estimates supplied by him:

1   Opening cash at bank balance 1 January £1,000.
2   An income tax payment amounting to £2,000 has to be made in January.
3   Arrangements have been made to purchase a new vehicle in March at a cost of £4,000.
4   Personal drawings of A. Smith amount to £500 per month.
5   To provide additional finance for the business A. Smith has agreed to contribute a further £3,000 which he will pay into the business in February.
6   There were creditors outstanding at 1 January amounting to £4,000. All creditors are paid in the month following purchases.
7   The credit sales in October, November and December were £5,000, £6,500 and £8,000 respectively. It has been Mr Smith's experience that debtors pay as follows:
      20% in the first month after the sale
      60% in the second month after the sale
      20% in the third month after the sale.
8   Mr Smith has estimated sales, purchases and other expenses for January to March as:

	Sales		Purchases		Other expenses
	Cash	Credit	Cash	Credit	
	£	£	£	£	£
Jan	2,000	4,000	1,500	4,000	1,000
Feb	1,500	4,000	2,000	4,500	1,500
Mar	5,000	5,000	3,000	4,000	2,000

Note   Other expenses are paid during the month in which they are incurred.

From the foregoing a cash forecast is to be prepared for the three months, January to March, as shown opposite.

Information to be included in cash forecast

☐   Total estimated cash receipts for period.
☐   Total estimated cash expenditure for period.
☐   Adjustments in respect of estimated cash/bank balances for period.
☐   Overall estimated surplus/deficit in cash for period.

156

A. SMITH
Cash forecast for three months   *January – March*

	January £	February £	March £
Estimated receipts			
Cash sales	2,000	1,500	5,000
Amounts received from debtors	6,500	6,900	4,800
Capital paid in by proprietor		3,000	
Total estimated receipts	8,500	11,400	9,800
Estimated payments			
Cash purchases	1,500	2,000	3,000
Amounts paid to creditors	4,000	4,000	4,500
Other expenses	1,000	1,500	2,000
Income tax	2,000		
Purchase of vehicle			4,000
Personal drawings	500	500	500
Total estimated payments	9,000	8,000	14,000
Bank balance at start month	1,000	500	3,900
Excess of receipts over payments (net inflow)		3,400	
Excess of payments over receipts (net outflow)	500		4,200
Bank balance at end of month	500	3,900	300 o/d

WORKING NOTES
Schedule of cash paid to creditors

	January £	February £	March £
Based on previous month's purchases	4,000	4,000	4,500

The amounts paid in January, February and March will be the credit purchases made in December, January and February.

Schedule of cash received from debtors

Invoice date	Total £	November £	December £	January £	February £	March £
October	5,000	1,000	3,000	1,000		
November	6,500	—	1,300	3,900	1,300	
December	8,000	—	—	1,600	4,800	1,600
January	4,000	—	—	—	800	2,400
February	4,000	—	—	—	—	800
March	5,000	--	—	—	—	—
				6,500	6,900	4,800

The basis of cash received from debtors is:

In month following Invoice	20% of invoiced amount
In second month following Invoice	60% of invoiced amount
In third month following Invoice	20% of invoiced amount

19 How to Prepare a Source and Application of Funds Statement

Purpose

To establish how a business generates funds during the year and how it uses these funds to finance the various aspects of the business. To assist in the control of the liquidity of the business and to uncover the reasons for changes in the working capital position.

Difference between a 'funds statement' and a 'receipts and payments statement'

It is necessary to distinguish between the following statements:

1 *Receipts and payments statement*   This is a statement prepared on a periodic basis to reveal the total cash receipts and payments made by a business. It does not take into account any credit given or taken during the period under review.
2 *Funds statement*   This is a statement prepared on a periodic basis, usually annually, to disclose the net changes which have occurred between two balance sheets taking into account not only changes in the cash position but also in all other items in the balance sheet including the profit earned in the period.

Main sources of funds in a business

Profit on trading operations.
Depreciation.
Additional capital introduced.
Proceeds from sale of fixed assets.
Decrease in stock, debtors, cash at bank and other current assets.
Increase in creditors, bank overdraft and other current liabilities.

Main application of funds

Loss in trading operations.
Purchase of fixed assets.
Repayment of loans and other long-term liabilities.
Proprietor's or partner's drawings.
Payment of dividends to shareholders.
Payment of taxation.
Increase in stock, debtors, cash at bank and other current assets.
Decrease in creditors, bank overdraft and other current liabilities.

Basic principles of source and application of funds statement

Sources of funds are provided from:

a   An increase in a liability, e.g. additional loan.
b   A decrease in an asset, e.g. reduction in stock.

Application of funds occur when there is:

a   A reduction in a liability, e.g. reduction in creditors.
b   An increase in an asset, e.g. purchase of fixed assets.

158

Information obtained from statement

Fixed assets bought or sold.
New capital introduced into the business.
Repayments of loans.
Profit for the period.
Changes in the working capital position.

Structure of statement

	£	£	£
A. SMITH LTD			
Statement of source and application of funds			
Source of funds			
Profit before taxation			X
Adjustment for items not involving the movement of funds:			X
Depreciation			X
Total generated from operations			X
Funds from other sources			
Issue of shares for cash			X
			X
Application of funds			
Dividends paid		X	
Tax paid		X	
Purchase of fixed assets		X	X
			X
Increase/decrease in working capital			
Stocks		X	
Debtors		X	
Creditors		X	
Movements in liquid funds:			
Cash balances	X		
Short-term investments	X	X	X

Note A similar type of structure can be used for a sole proprietor or a partnership business. Taxation, Dividends paid and Issue of Shares would not be shown in such statements.

Illustration ### Steps in the preparation of a source and application of funds statement

Step 1

This is a simple example showing the net changes in each item between Year 1 and Year 2 in the balance sheets of A. Smith Ltd.

Summarised balance sheet of A. Smith Ltd			
	Year 1 £	Year 2 £	Change £
Assets			
Land and buildings	20,000	20,000	—
Plant	5,000	7,000	+2,000
Motor vehicles	7,000	8,000	+1,000
Stock	10,000	9,000	−1,000
Debtors	15,000	18,000	+3,000
Cash	400	300	− 100
	57,400	62,300	+4,900
Liabilities			
Owners' capital	30,000	40,000	+10,000
Profit and loss account	9,000	11,000	+ 2,000
Creditors	7,000	4,000	− 3,000
Bank overdraft	11,400	7,300	− 4,100
	57,400	62,300	+ 4,900

From the above statement and following the information given under the section 'Main Sources of Funds' and 'Application of Funds' a simple form of funds statement can be prepared showing the changes in the balance sheets between Years 1 and 2.

Step 2

The statement below has been prepared simply by showing the changes between the balance sheets and discloses where funds came from and to what purpose they were used.

Statement of source and application of funds between years 1 and 2	
	£
Source of funds	
Increase in profit and loss account	2,000
Increase in share capital	10,000
Decrease in stock	1,000
Decrease in cash	100
	13,100
Application of funds	
Increase in plant	2,000
Increase in motor vehicles	1,000
Increase in debtors	3,000
Decrease in creditors	3,000
Decrease in bank overdraft	4,100
	13,100

Step 3

The Statement of Source and Application of Funds can now be shown in the conventional form as shown under the structure of a Statement of Source and Application of Funds.

A. SMITH LTD
Statement of source and application of funds for year 2

		£	£	£
Source of funds				
Profit for year				2,000
Total generated from operations				2,000
Funds from other sources:				
Issue of shares				10,000
				12,000
Application of funds				
Purchase of fixed assets:	Plant		2,000	
	Motor vehicles		1,000	3,000
				9,000
Increase in working capital				
Decrease in creditors			3,000	
Increase in debtors			3,000	
			6,000	
Less: Decrease in stock			1,000	
			5,000	
Movements in net liquid funds				
Decrease in bank overdraft		4,100		
Less: Increase in cash		100	4,000	9,000

The effect on working capital of changes in current assets and current liabilities

Increases in current assets	increase working capital
Decreases in current assets	decrease working capital
Increases in current liabilities	decrease working capital
Decreases in current liabilities	increase working capital

Net increase	in working capital is an	application of funds
Decrease	in working capital is a	source of funds

Preparation of cash flow statement from source and application of funds statement

Using the information from the previous example, the following statement can be prepared; this explains the reason for the decrease in the cash and bank position during Year 2:

A. SMITH LTD
Cash flow statement for Year 2

	Source £	Application £	£	£
Bank overdraft at start of Year 2			11,000	
Less: Cash in hand			400	11,000
Net source of funds per statement	9,000			
Stock decrease	1,000			
Creditors decrease		3,000		
Debtors increase		3,000		
	10,000	6,000		4,000
Bank overdraft at end of Year 2			7,300	
Less: Cash in hand			300	7,000

Working capital

What is it?

Working capital is the difference between current assets and current liabilities.

The flow of working capital

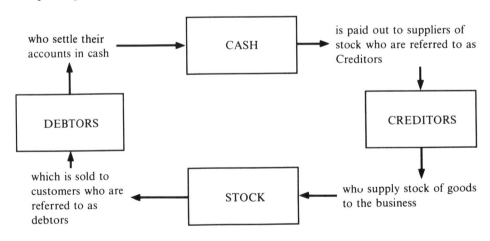

Importance of working capital

☐ The working capital of a business reflects its financial health.
☐ Inadequate working capital in a business will mean that it will be unable to meet its debts as they fall due and eventually will run the risk of bankruptcy.
☐ It is essential that every business ensures that adequate levels of working capital are maintained if the business is to remain in existence and also be able to expand its activities.

Controlling working capital

Management of working capital involves:

1 *Control of stock*   This is achieved by operating an efficient stock control system where maximum and minimum stock levels are established and adequate controls are in existence for the receipt and issue of stocks so reducing pilferage and obsolete stocks.
2 *Control of debtors*   This is achieved by ensuring that there is in operation an efficient and speedy system of invoicing goods to customers and obtaining payment from them within pre-determined credit limits.
3 *Control of creditors*   This is obtained by ensuring that there is an effective system of recording and checking suppliers' invoices. It is also essential that cash is available to meet debts as they fall due so that discounts can be obtained for prompt payment.
4 *Control of cash*   This is achieved by preparation of cash forecasts to ensure that adequate arrangements are made beforehand to meet the debts which fall due in the accounting period. This forecast has to be monitored constantly during the period to verify that the actual position is in line with that forecast.

Part 5 The Kalamazoo Bookkeeping System for Small Businesses

The Kalamazoo Bookkeeping System for Small Businesses

Purpose

□ To introduce the businessman to a basic system of accounting, using the principles set out in Parts 1–3 of this book, that will enable him to record his financial transactions according to a simple and easy-to-follow method.

□ The information contained in this Part of the book forms the instruction manual for the Kalamazoo Bookkeeping System for Small Businesses.

Main features

The Kalamazoo Bookkeeping System for Small Businesses provides the businessman with an accounting system that will enable him to record the following business transactions:

□ Customers' credit sales.
□ Credit notes sent to customers.
□ Invoices received from suppliers.
□ Credit notes received from suppliers.
□ Cheque receipts and payments.
□ Petty cash payments.
□ VAT due to or from Customs and Excise.

Advantages of the system

□ It provides the basic accounting records to the businessman for recording his financial transactions.

□ There are simple and easy-to-follow instructions given which can be understood and applied by businessmen or their staff who have little or no knowledge of bookkeeping.

□ The recording of each business transaction is shown step-by-step.

□ Fully illustrated examples are shown for each business transaction and cross-referenced to the recording instructions and to the appropriate text of the book.

□ The accounting system has been designed by Kalamazoo Business Systems who are the market leaders in the design and manufacture of business systems.

□ If the system is kept up-to-date it will provide essential information for the efficient and successful running of the business.

□ By the use of the simple technique of recording the old balance, i.e. the amount previously owing or outstanding, each transaction is self-balancing.

Contents of the system

Stationery

For recording credit sales

Yellow Ledger Cards – for recording credit transactions for each customer.

Customers' Statements – for advising customers how much they owe.

Sales Day Book Sheets – for recording details of all credit sales.

Sales Returns Day Book Sheets – for recording details of returns from customers.

Cash Journal Sheets – for recording all payments received from customers.

Sales Ledger Control Account Sheets – for recording in total the amount due from customers.

Age Analysis Sheets – for recording the age of each amount owed by customers.

For recording credit purchases

Green Ledger Cards – for recording transactions with each supplier.

Purchases Day Book Sheets – for recording details of all credit purchases.

Purchases Returns Day Book Sheets – for recording details of all returns to suppliers.

Payments Journal Sheets – for recording all payments made to suppliers.

Purchase Ledger Control Account Sheets – for recording in total the amount due to suppliers.

For recording receipts and payments by cheque

General Cash Book Receipts section – for recording the amount received from customers in total and other sources of income.

General Cash Book Payments section – for recording the amount paid to suppliers in total and all other payments by cheque.

For recording small cash payments

Petty Cash Book Sheets – for recording the amounts paid out by the business for small expense items.

For recording VAT

VAT Summary Sheets – for recording the amount of VAT due to or from Customs and Excise.

Other equipment

Kalamazoo Folder Tray – used for storing the ledger cards.

Blue Kalamazoo Binder – used for storing stationery used in the Set-up Pack.

White Plastic Collator – used for ensuring uniformity in recording transactions on ledger cards and statements (see instructions for using).

How to use the white plastic collator

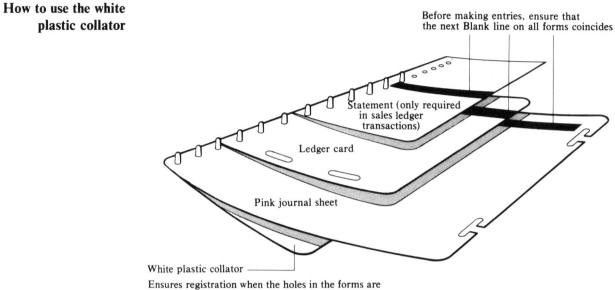

Before making entries, ensure that the next Blank line on all forms coincides

Statement (only required in sales ledger transactions)

Ledger card

Pink journal sheet

White plastic collator

Ensures registration when the holes in the forms are placed over the protruding cones as shown

How to assemble and use the folder tray

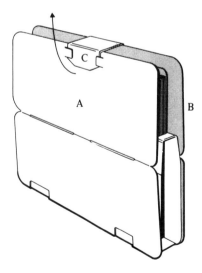

1 Pull securing flap C in direction indicated to open folder

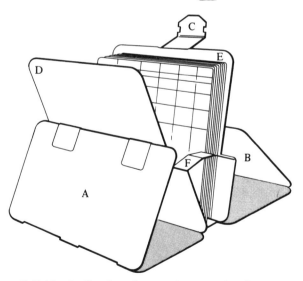

2 Fold outer flap A as shown and secure using the two retaining tags in inner flap D

3 Fold outer flap B in the same way and secure using the two retaining tags in inner flap E

4 Press down side restraints F to ensure that folder tray is flat on table, and place ledger cards in the 'V'

Accounting for credit sales

Preparing a yellow ledger card for each customer

Procedure

Head up a Yellow Ledger Card for each customer in the following manner:

DATE	REF. NO.	DETAILS	VAT		DEBIT		CREDIT		BALANCE		OLD BALANCE	
④		Bal B/Fwd							73	40		
Sept 18	900	Goods	6	67	66	70			146	77	73	40
Sept 25	519	Cash					73	40	73	37	146	77

NAME WARD & Co LTD ACCOUNT NO. W1
ADDRESS LONG ROW, CALNE, WILTS, SN11 001 CR. £500 ③

Example 1

Key

1 Name and address of customer.
2 Account number.
3 Credit limit.
4 Details of transaction.

Preparing a statement for each customer

Procedure

Head up a Statement for each customer in the following manner:

① A. SMITH									
GENERAL WHOLESALER									

② Ward + Co Ltd
Long Row, Calne
Wilts
5N11 001

Anytown
England
Tel : ANY 500

③ DATE – Sept. 30

④ DATE	REF. NO.	DETAILS	VAT		DEBIT		CREDIT		BALANCE	
Sept 1		A/c Rendered							73	40
Sept 18	900	Goods	6	67	66	70			146	77
Sept 25	519	Cash					73	40	73	37

Example 2

Key

1 Name and address of your business.
2 Name and address of customer.
3 Date of Statement.
4 Details of transactions.

Changing to the Kalamazoo bookkeeping system for small businesses from your present system

This section is, of course, not applicable if you are starting up a new business.

Example

A. Smith has the following balances outstanding in his old sales ledger:

Customer	Old balance
	£
Abbott Ltd	23.28
Benton Ltd	30.00
Browning & Co.	2,582.31
Harding Ltd	986.45
Nor Petrol	100.00
M.D. Enterprises	3,275.41
Ward & Co. Ltd	73.40

Procedure

Step 1   Pre-list the balances on the sales ledger as follows:

£23.28 + £30.00 + £2,582.31 + £986.45 + £100.00 + £3,275.41 + £73.40 = £7,070.85.

Step 2   Head up the first page in the 'SALES' section 'Journal of Opening Entries'. Using the collator as illustrated, transfer the balances to the appropriate Statements and Yellow Ledger Cards, over the pink Journal of Opening Entries, as shown in Example 3.

Step 3   Check that all the balances have been brought forward on to the Statements, Ledger Cards and Journal of Opening Entries.

Total column 7 = Pre-list total

Step 4   Record the total balances (column 7 total) in the Sales Ledger Control Account as shown in Example 4.

Page		JOURNAL OF OPENING ENTRIES							
① Date	② Ref. No.	③	④	⑤ Debit	⑥ Credit	⑦ Balance	⑧ Old Balance	⑨ Account	
		Brought Forward							
Sept 1		A/c Rendered				23 28		Abbott Ltd	
Sept 1		A/c Rendered				30 00		Benton Ltd	
Sept 1		A/c Rendered				2582 31		Browning & Co	
Sept 1		A/c Rendered				986 45		Harding Ltd	
Sept 1		A/c Rendered				100 00		Nor Petrol	
Sept 1		A/c Rendered				3275 41		M.D. Enterprises	
Sept 1		A/c Rendered				73 40		Ward & Co	
						7070 85			

Example 3

SALES Ledger Control Account

Date	Ref.	Details	Debits	Credits	Balance	
Sept 1		Brought Forward			7070	85

Example 4

173

Recording sales invoices sent to customers

Example

A. Smith sends the following sales invoices to customers:

Date	Invoice no.	Customer	Goods ex VAT	VAT	Old balance
			£	£	£
Sep 18	900	Ward & Co. Ltd	66.70	6.67	73.40
Sep 18	901	Benton Ltd	161.84	11.33	30.00
Sep 18	902	Nor Petrol	117.48	8.26	100.00
Sep 18	903	Abbott Ltd	177.26	16.03	23.28
			523.28	42.29	

Procedure

Step 1 Select Sales Day Book Sheet which is located behind the Index Tab 'SALES' in the blue binder.

Step 2 Pre-list the batch of sales invoices to be recorded: £523.28 + £42.29 = £565.57

Step 3 Position the collator behind the Sales Day Book Page. Select the first customer's statement and ledger card (Ward & Co. Ltd) and align them over the Day Book Page as illustrated. Record Sales Invoices in the Sales Day Book and Ledger Cards and Statements as shown in Example 5.

Step 4 Check that Sales Invoices have been correctly entered in the Sales Day Book, Ledger Accounts and Statements.

Column 4 + Column 5 = Pre-list total
£42.29 + £523.28 = £565.57

Column 4 + Column 5 + Column 8 = Column 7
£42.29 + £523.28 + £226.68 = £792.25

Step 5 Record total of Goods Value + VAT (Column 5 + Column 4) in Sales Ledger Control Account – see Example 6.

Step 6 Record total Goods Value and total VAT separately in the VAT Summary – see Example 7.

Step 7 File copy Invoices in order of entry in Sales Day Book.

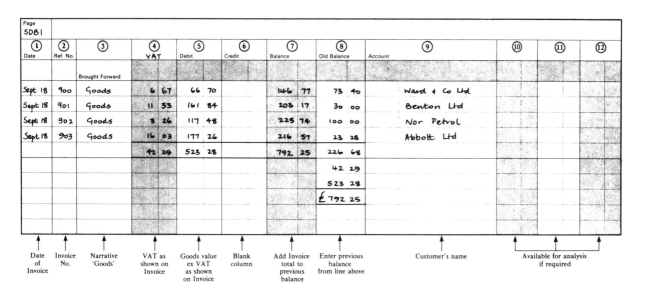

Page SDB1											
① Date	② Ref. No.	③	④ VAT	⑤ Debit	⑥ Credit	⑦ Balance	⑧ Old Balance	⑨ Account	⑩	⑪	⑫
		Brought Forward									
Sept 18	900	Goods	6 67	66 70		146 77	73 40	Ward & Co Ltd			
Sept 18	901	Goods	11 33	161 84		203 17	30 00	Benton Ltd			
Sept 18	902	Goods	8 26	117 48		225 74	100 00	Nor Petrol			
Sept 18	903	Goods	16 03	177 26		216 57	23 28	Abbott Ltd			
			42 29	523 28		792 25	226 68				
							42 29				
							523 28				
							£792 25				

Date of Invoice | Invoice No. | Narrative 'Goods' | VAT as shown on Invoice | Goods value ex VAT as shown on Invoice | Blank column | Add Invoice total to previous balance | Enter previous balance from line above | Customer's name | Available for analysis if required

Example 5

SALES		Ledger Control Account				
Date	Ref.	Details	Debits	Credits	Balance	
Sept 1		Brought Forward			7070	85
Sept 18	SDB1	Sales incl. VAT	565 57		7636	42

Example 6

VAT Summary			Period from *1 September* to *30 November*				Bold Figures refer to appropriate Boxes on Quarterly VAT Return (VAT 100)				
Tax Due				Outputs		Tax Deductible			Inputs		
Date	Ref.	Details	Output Tax	Output Values (Sales etc.)		Date	Ref.	Details	Input Tax	Input Values (Purchases etc.)	
		Brought Forward									
Sept 18	SDB1	Sales	42 29	523 28							

Example 7

175

Recording payments received from credit customers

Example

A. Smith receives the following payments from customers:

Date	Customer	Ref.	Amount received	Discount	Old balance
			£		£
Sep 25	Abbott Ltd	306	22.60	0.38	216.57
Sep 25	Benton Ltd	415	50.00	3.25	203.17
Sep 25	Nor Petrol	618	100.00	—	225.74
Sep 25	Ward & Co. Ltd	519	73.40	—	146.77

Procedure

Step 1   Receipts are recorded on the Cash Journal, a subsidiary Journal of the General Cash Book. You will find the Cash Journal behind the Orange Index Tab marked 'RECEIPTS'.

Step 2   Arrange cheques in alphabetical order.

Step 3   List the customers' names and the amount of their payment in Columns 9 and 10 in the Cash Journal Sheet. Record any discount in Column 11.

Step 4   Position the collator behind the Cash Journal Sheet. Select the first customer's Ledger Card and Statement (Abbott Ltd) and align them over the Cash Journal. Make the entries through all three forms as shown in Example 8.

Step 5   Check that the customers' payments have been recorded correctly in the Cash Journal Sheet, Ledger Cards and Statements as follows:

Column 6 = Column 10 + Column 11
£249.63 = £246.00 + £3.63

Column 8 – Column 6 = Column 7
£792.25 – £249.63 = £542.62

Step 6   Record total customers' *credits* (Column 6) in Sales Ledger Control Account – see Example 9.

Step 7   Record total Customers' *payments* (Column 10) in Receipts side of General Cash Book – see Example 10.

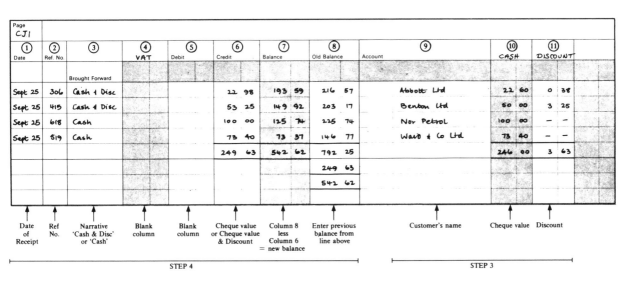

Page CJI	① Date	② Ref. No.	③	④ VAT	⑤ Debit	⑥ Credit	⑦ Balance	⑧ Old Balance	⑨ Account	⑩ CASH	⑪ DISCOUNT
			Brought Forward								
	Sept 25	306	Cash & Disc			22 98	193 59	216 57	Abbott Ltd	22 60	0 38
	Sept 25	415	Cash & Disc			53 25	149 92	203 17	Benton Ltd	50 00	3 25
	Sept 25	618	Cash			100 00	125 74	225 74	Nor Petrol	100 00	— —
	Sept 25	519	Cash			73 40	73 37	146 77	Ward & Co Ltd	73 40	— —
						249 63	542 62	792 25		246 00	3 63
								249 63			
								542 62			

| Date of Receipt | Ref No. | Narrative 'Cash & Disc' or 'Cash' | Blank column | Blank column | Cheque value or Cheque value & Discount | Column 8 less Column 6 = new balance | Enter previous balance from line above | Customer's name | Cheque value | Discount |

STEP 4 — STEP 3

Example 8

SALES		Ledger Control Account					
Date	Ref.	Details	Debits		Credits		Balance
Sept 1		Brought Forward					7070 85
Sept 18	SDB1	Sales incl VAT	565 57				7636 42
Sept 25	CJI	Cash & Discount			249 63		7386 79

Example 9

	RECEIPTS									PAYMENTS					
DATE	DETAILS	FOL.	SALES LEDGER						DATE	DETAILS	FOL.	1	2	3	
	BROUGHT FWD									BROUGHT FWD					
Sept 25	Credit Sales	CJI	246 00												

Example 10

Recording credit notes sent to credit customers

Example

A. Smith sends the following credit notes to customers:

Date	Customer	Credit note no.	Value ex VAT	VAT	Old balance
			£	£	£
Sep 29	Abbott Ltd	36	15.20	2.28	193.59
Sep 29	Benton Ltd	37	9.10	1.36	149.92
			24.30	3.64	

Procedure

Step 1 Credit notes are recorded in the Sales Returns Day Book which is found behind the orange index tab marked 'RETURNS'.

Step 2 Pre-list the batch of credit notes to be recorded £24.30 + £3.64 = £27.94.

Step 3 Position the collator behind the Sales Returns Day Book. By aligning the appropriate Customer's Ledger Card and Statement over the Day Book, record the credit notes on all three forms together as in Example 11.

Step 4 Check that the credit notes have been entered correctly in the Sales Returns Day Book, Ledger Cards and Statements as follows:

Column 4 + Column 6 = Pre-list
£3.64 + £24.30 = £27.94

Column 4 + Column 6 + Column 7 = Column 8
£3.64 + £24.30 + £315.57 = £343.51

Step 5 Record the total of credit note value and VAT in the Sales Ledger Control Account – see Example 12.

Step 6 Record the Goods Value Total and VAT total separately in the VAT Summary – see Example 13.

Step 7 File copy credit notes in strict order of entry in the Sales Returns Day Book.

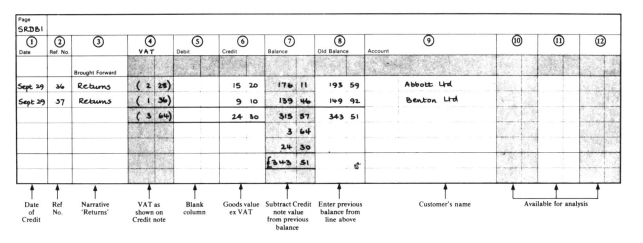

Page SRDB1												
① Date	② Ref. No.	③	④ VAT	⑤ Debit	⑥ Credit	⑦ Balance	⑧ Old Balance	⑨ Account		⑩	⑪	⑫
		Brought Forward										
Sept 29	36	Returns	(2 28)		15 20	176 11	193 59	Abbott Ltd				
Sept 29	37	Returns	(1 36)		9 10	139 46	149 92	Benton Ltd				
			(3 64)		24 30	315 57	343 51					
						3 64						
						24 30						
						£343 51						

Date of Credit — Ref No. — Narrative 'Returns' — VAT as shown on Credit note — Blank column — Goods value ex VAT — Subtract Credit note value from previous balance — Enter previous balance from line above — Customer's name — Available for analysis

Example 11

SALES	Ledger Control Account							
Date	Ref.	Details		Debits		Credits		Balance
Sept 1		Brought Forward						7070 85
Sept 18	SDB1	Sales and VAT		565 57				7636 42
Sept 25	CJ1	Cash and Discount				249 63		7386 79
Sept 29	SRDB1	Sales Returns				27 94		7358 85

Example 12

VAT Summary			Period from 1 September to 30 November					
Tax Due					Outputs	Tax Deductible		
Date	Ref.	Details	Output Tax		Output Values (Sales etc.)	Date	Ref.	Details
		Brought Forward						
Sept 18	SDB1	Sales	42	29	523 28			
Sept 29	SRDB1	Sales Returns	(3	64)	(24 30)			

Example 13

179

Preparing a new statement for each customer and controlling the amount of credit taken by your customers — age analysis and credit control

Example

The following balances are outstanding on A. Smith's Sales Ledger Cards at the end of September:

Customer	Balance	Current month	1 month	2 month	3 month
	£	£	£	£	£
Abbott Ltd	176.11	176.11	—	—	—
Benton Ltd	139.46	139.46	—	—	—
Browning & Co.	2,582.31	—	82.86	189.50	2,309.95
Harding Ltd	986.45	—	986.45	—	—
Nor Petrol	125.74	125.74	—	—	—
M.D. Enterprises	3,275.41	—	1,380.20	1,456.00	439.21
Ward & Co. Ltd	73.37	73.37	—	—	—
	7,358.85	514.68	2,449.51	1,645.50	2,749.16

Procedure

Step 1 Statements are sent monthly, and new ones prepared. The balance for each customer is recorded in the 'DEBTORS' AGE ANALYSIS' section in the blue binder.

Step 2 Pre-list balances on Sales Ledger Cards as follows:

£176.11 + £139.46 + £2,582.31 + £986.45 + £125.74 + £3,275.41 + £73.37 = £7,358.85.

Step 3 Position the collator behind the Debtors' Age Analysis Page. Head-up a new statement for the first customer (Abbott Ltd) and align it over the Debtors' Age Analysis Journal using the collator. Copy the account balance from the old Statement to the new. Repeat until all balances have been transferred – see Example 14.

Step 4 Check that all the balances have been brought forward correctly to the new Statements.

Total Column 4 = Pre-list total.

Step 5 Refer to each Customer's Ledger Card in turn and age analyse the balance on the Debtor's Age Analysis Journal – see Example 15.

Step 6 Place new statements in front of appropriate customer's Ledger Card and post old statements to customers.

Step 7 Use the list of debtors to decide on further action. For example, £2,749.16 owed from 3 months ago – send reminder letters and stop further credit for Browning & Co. and M.D. Enterprises.

Age Analysis SEPTEMBER

Date	Ref. No.	Details	Account Balance	Account No.	Account Name
		Brought Forward			
Sept 30		A/c Rendered	176 11		Abbott Ltd
Sept 30		A/c Rendered	139 46		Benton Ltd
Sept 30		A/c Rendered	2582 31		Browning + Co
Sept 30		A/c Rendered	986 45		Harding Ltd
Sept 30		A/c Rendered	125 74		Nor Petrol
Sept 30		A/c Rendered	3275 41		M.D. Enterprises
Sept 30		A/c Rendered	73 37		Ward + Co Ltd
			£7358 85		

Example 14

Outstanding

	Current	1	2	3	4
1	176.11				
2	139.46				
3		82.86	189.50	2309.95	
4		986.45			
5	125.74				
6		1380.20	1456.00	439.21	
7	73.37				
8	514.68	2449.51	1645.50	2749.16	
9					
10					

Example 15

Accounting for credit purchases

Preparing a green ledger card for each supplier

Procedure

Head up a Green Ledger Card for each supplier in the following manner:

DATE	REF. NO.	DETAILS	VAT		DEBIT		CREDIT		BALANCE		OLD BALANCE	
Sept 1		Bal. B/F							227	44		
Sept 12	799	Goods	3	35			33	50	264	29	227	44
Sept 15	81	Cash			227	44			36	85	264	29
Sept 19	85	Returns	(3	00)	20	00			13	85	36	85

NAME ANDERSON + CO ACCOUNT NO. A17
ADDRESS HIGH STREET, BARCHESTER, LANCS CR. £600

Example 16

Key

1 Name and address of supplier.
2 Account number.
3 Credit limit.
4 Details of transactions.

Changing to the Kalamazoo book-keeping system for small businesses from your present system

This section is, of course, not applicable if you are starting up a new business.

Example

A. Smith has the following balances outstanding in his old purchases ledger:

Supplier	Old balance
	£
Anderson & Co.	227.44
Johnson Electronics	1,287.25
Multiwrite Ltd	582.39
Plastic Co. Ltd	70.00
Screw Co. Ltd	39.61
Storry Ltd	169.59
M. Waters & Son	1,213.97

Procedure

Step 1 Pre-list the balances on your Purchases Ledger as follows:

£227.44 + £1,287.25 + £582.39 + £70.00 + £39.61 + £169.59 + £1,213.97 = £3,590.25.

Step 2 Head up the first page in the 'PURCHASES' section of the blue binder 'Journal of Opening Entries'. Using the collator transfer the balances to the appropriate Green Ledger cards over the Journal of opening entries – see Example 17.

Step 3 Check that all the balances have been brought forward on to the Suppliers' Ledger Cards and Journal of Opening Entries correctly.

Total Column 7 = Pre-list total

Step 4 Record the total balances (Column 7 total) in the Purchases Ledger Control Account – see Example 18.

Page	② Ref. No.	③	④	⑤ Debit	⑥ Credit	⑦ Balance	⑧ Old Balance	⑨ Account
① Date								
		JOURNAL OF OPENING ENTRIES						
		Brought Forward						
Sept 1		Bal B|F				227 44		Anderson & Co
Sept 1		Bal B|F				1287 25		Johnson Electronics
Sept 1		Bal B|F				582 39		Multiconite Ltd
Sept 1		Bal B|F				70 00		Plastic Co Ltd
Sept 1		Bal B|F				39 61		Screw Co Ltd
Sept 1		Bal B|F				169 59		Storry Ltd
Sept 1		Bal B|F				1213 97		M. Waters & Son
						£3590 25		

Example 17

PURCHASES Ledger Control Account

Date	Ref.	Details	Debits		Credits		Balance	
Sept 1		Brought Forward					3590	25

Example 18

Recording invoices received from suppliers

Example

A. Smith receives the following invoices from suppliers:

Date	Supplier	Invoice no.	Goods ex VAT	VAT	Old balance
			£	£	£
Sep 12	Anderson & Co.	799	33.50	3.35	227.44
Sep 12	Screw Co. Ltd	173	6.78	0.68	39.61
Sep 12	Plastic Co. Ltd	495	77.50	7.75	70.00
Sep 12	Storry Ltd	654	138.17	13.82	169.59
			255.95	25.60	

Procedure

Step 1 Purchases invoices are recorded in the Purchases Day Book. Select the Purchases Day Book Sheet which is located behind the Index Tab 'PURCHASES' in the blue binder.

Step 2 Pre-list the batch of invoices to be recorded in the Purchases Day Book as follows:

£255.95 + £25.60 = £281.55

Step 3 Position the collator behind the Purchases Day Book. Select the first Supplier's Green Ledger card (Anderson & Co.) and align it over the Purchases Day Book using the collator and make the entries through both forms – see Example 19.

Step 4 Check that the suppliers' invoices have been correctly entered in the Purchases Day Book and Ledger Cards as follows:

Column 4 + Column 6 = Pre-list total
£25.60 + £255.95 = £281.55

Column 4 + Column 6 + Column 8 = Column 7
£25.60 + £255.95 + £506.64 = £788.19

Step 5 Record total of Goods Value and VAT (Column 6 + Column 4) in Purchases Ledger Control Account – see Example 20.

Step 6 Record Total Goods Value and total VAT separately in VAT Summary – see Example 21.

Step 7 File suppliers' invoices in strict order of entry in Purchases Day Book.

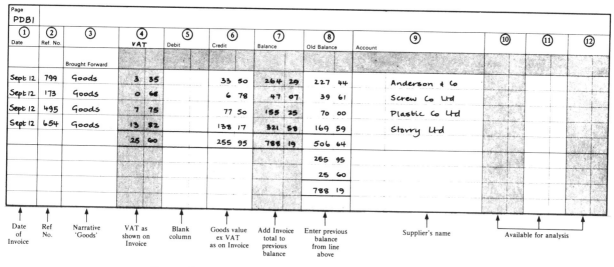

Page PDB1											
① Date	② Ref. No.	③	④ VAT	⑤ Debit	⑥ Credit	⑦ Balance	⑧ Old Balance	⑨ Account	⑩	⑪	⑫
		Brought Forward									
Sept 12	799	Goods	3 35		33 50	264 29	227 44	Anderson & Co			
Sept 12	173	Goods	0 68		6 78	47 07	39 61	Screw Co Ltd			
Sept 12	495	Goods	7 75		77 50	155 25	70 00	Plastic Co Ltd			
Sept 12	654	Goods	13 82		138 17	321 58	169 59	Storry Ltd			
			25 60		255 95	788 19	506 64				
							255 95				
							25 60				
							788 19				

Date of Invoice — Ref No. — Narrative 'Goods' — VAT as shown on Invoice — Blank column — Goods value ex VAT as on Invoice — Add Invoice total to previous balance — Enter previous balance from line above — Supplier's name — Available for analysis

Example 19

PURCHASES		Ledger Control Account				
Date	Ref.	Details	Debits	Credits		Balance
Sept 1		Brought Forward				3590 25
Sept 12	PDB1	Purchases incl. VAT		281 55		3871 80

Example 20

VAT Summary			Period from 1 September to 30 November			Bold Figures refer to appropriate Boxes on Quarterly VAT Return (VAT 100)				
Tax Due				Outputs		Tax Deductible			Inputs	
Date	Ref.	Details	Output Tax	Output Values (Sales etc.)		Date	Ref.	Details	Input Tax	Input Values (Purchases etc.)
		Brought Forward								
						Sept 12	PDB1	Purchases	25 60	255 95

Example 21

Recording payments made to suppliers

Example

A. Smith pays the following suppliers:

Date	Supplier	Ref.	Cheque amount	Discount	Old balance
			£	£	£
Sep 15	Anderson & Co.	81	227.44	—	264.29
Sep 15	Screw Co. Ltd	82	38.55	1.06	47.07
Sep 15	Plastic Co. Ltd	83	70.00	—	155.25
Sep 15	Storry Ltd	84	165.50	4.09	321.58

Procedure

Step 1 Payments to suppliers are recorded on the Payments Journal Sheets which are located behind the Index Tab 'PAYMENTS' in the blue binder.

Step 2 Write out cheque for each supplier remembering to deduct any discount allowed.

Step 3 List payment made to each supplier and discount received from them in Payments Journal Sheet (Columns 9, 10 and 11).

Step 4 Total Cash and Discount columns. Total Cash column should agree with total cheques issued.

Step 5 Position the collator behind the Payments Journal Sheet. Select the Green Ledger Card for the first Supplier on the list of payees (Column 9) and align over the Payments Journal and make the entries through both forms as in Example 22.

Step 6 Check that the payments have been correctly recorded in the Ledger Accounts and Payments Journal Sheet as follows:

Column 8 – Column 5 = Column 7
£788.19 – £506.64 = £281.55

Step 7 Record the total payments and discount in the Purchases Ledger Control Account – see Example 23.

Step 8 Record the total payments, i.e. cheque amounts only, on the payments side of the General Cash Book – see Example 24.

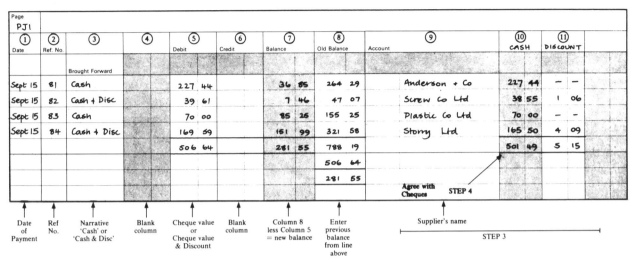

Page PJ1	① Date	② Ref. No.	③	④	⑤ Debit	⑥ Credit	⑦ Balance	⑧ Old Balance	⑨ Account	⑩ CASH	⑪ DISCOUNT	
			Brought Forward									
	Sept 15	81	Cash		227 44		36 85	264 29	Anderson + Co	227 44	— —	
	Sept 15	82	Cash + Disc		39 61		7 46	47 07	Screw Co Ltd	38 55	1 06	
	Sept 15	83	Cash		70 00		85 25	155 25	Plastic Co Ltd	70 00	— —	
	Sept 15	84	Cash + Disc		169 59		151 99	321 58	Storry Ltd	165 50	4 09	
					506 64		281 55	788 19		501 49	5 15	
								506 64				
								281 55		Agree with Cheques STEP 4		

Date of Payment | Ref No. | Narrative 'Cash' or 'Cash & Disc' | Blank column | Cheque value or Cheque value & Discount | Blank column | Column 8 less Column 5 = new balance | Enter previous balance from line above | Supplier's name | STEP 3

Example 22

PURCHASES	Ledger Control Account								
Date	Ref.	Details			Debits		Credits		Balance	
			Brought Forward						3590	25
Sept 1										
Sept 12	PDB 1	Purchases in VAT					281	55	3871	80
Sept 15	PJ1	Cash and Discount			506	64			3365	16

Example 23

RECEIPTS							PAYMENTS						
DATE	DETAILS	FOL.					DATE	DETAILS	FOL.	1 PURCHASES LEDGER	2	3	
	BROUGHT FWD							BROUGHT FWD					
							Sept 12	Credit Purchases	PJ1	501 49			

Example 24

Recording credit notes received from suppliers

Example

A. Smith receives the following credit notes:

Date	Supplier	Credit note no.	Value ex VAT	VAT	Old balance
			£	£	£
Sep 19	Anderson & Co.	85	20.00	3.00	36.85
Sep 19	Storry Ltd	95	11.90	1.78	151.99
			31.90	4.78	

Procedure

Step 1 Credit notes from suppliers are recorded in the Purchases Returns Day Book which is located behind the *Black* Index tab marked 'RETURNS'.

Step 2 Pre-list the batch of credit notes to be recorded as follows:

£31.90 + £4.78 = £36.68.

Step 3 Position the collator behind the Purchases Returns Day Book. By aligning the first supplier's Ledger Card over the Day Book, record the credit note on both forms together as shown in Example 25.

Step 4 Check that the credit notes have been correctly entered in the Purchases Returns Day Book and Ledger Cards as follows:

Column 4 + Column 5 = Pre-list
£4.78 + £31.90 = £36.68

Column 4 + Column 5 + Column 7 = Column 8
£4.78 + £31.90 + £152.16 = £188.84

Step 5 Record the total of credit note values and VAT in the Purchases Ledger Control Account – see Example 26.

Step 6 Record the goods value total and VAT total separately in the VAT Summary – see Example 27.

Step 7 File credit notes in strict order of entry in Purchases Returns Day Book.

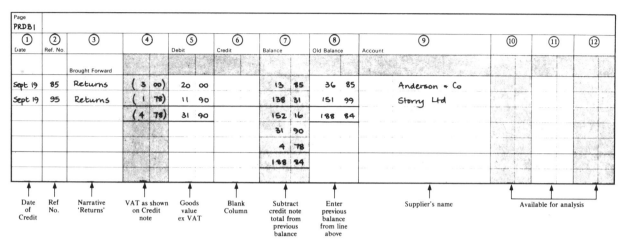

Page PRDB1											
① Date	② Ref. No.	③	④	⑤ Debit	⑥ Credit	⑦ Balance	⑧ Old Balance	⑨ Account	⑩	⑪	⑫
		Brought Forward									
Sept 19	85	Returns	(3 00)	20 00		13 85	36 85	Anderson & Co			
Sept 19	95	Returns	(1 78)	11 90		138 31	151 99	Storry Ltd			
			(4 78)	31 90		152 16	188 84				
						31 90					
						4 78					
						188 84					

Date of Credit — Ref No. — Narrative 'Returns' — VAT as shown on Credit note — Goods value ex VAT — Blank Column — Subtract credit note total from previous balance — Enter previous balance from line above — Supplier's name — Available for analysis

Example 25

PURCHASES		Ledger Control Account							
Date	Ref.	Details		Debits		Credits		Balance	
Sept 1		Brought Forward						3590	25
Sept 12	PDB1	Purchases incl. VAT				281	55	3871	80
Sept 15	PJ1	Cash and Discount		506	64			3365	16
Sept 19	PRDB1	Purchases Returns		36	68			3328	48

Example 26

VAT Summary			Period from 1 September to 30 November						Bold Figures refer to appropriate Boxes on Quarterly VAT Return (VAT 100)		
Tax Due						Outputs	Tax Deductible				Inputs
Date	Ref.	Details		Output Tax		Output Values (Sales etc.)	Date	Ref.	Details	Input Tax	Input Values (Purchases etc.)
		Brought Forward									
							Sept 12	PDB1	Purchases	25 60	255 95
							Sept 19	PRDB1	Purchases Returns	(4 78)	(31 90)

Example 27

General

Procedure

Step 1   Head up columns in the Cash Book as appropriate:

Receipts	*Payments*
Sales Ledger	Purchases Ledger
Other receipts	Petty cash
Balance	Wages
VAT (memorandum column)	Other payments
	Balance
	VAT (memorandum column)

Step 2   Enter opening balance in 'Balance' column, surpluses on the 'Receipts' side, deficits on the 'Payments' side.

Step 3   Enter items on 'Receipts' side of Cash Book as follows:

Source	Description	Column	VAT column
Cash journal sheets	Receipts from customers	Sales ledger	—
Other receipts	Amounts received which have not been already entered in cash journal sheets	Other receipts	Amount of VAT included in sum received

Step 4   Enter items on 'Payments' side of Cash Book as follows:

Source	Description	Column	VAT column
Payments journal sheets	Payments to suppliers	Purchases ledger	—
Petty cash book	Amount transferred to petty cash book	Petty cash	
Wages book	'Net' wages paid	Wages	—
Other payments	Amounts paid *not* already entered in the cash journal sheets, wages, or petty cash books	Other payments, *or* relevant analysis column	Amount of VAT included in payment

Step 5   Total columns and balance the Cash Book at the end of the month (see next section for balancing procedure). Enter Balance on:
   'Receipts' side balance column if a deficit
   'Payments' side balance column if a surplus
Do *not* include total of VAT columns when balancing the Cash Book.

Step 6   Update VAT Summary as follows:
   Transfer total of 'Receipts' VAT column to Tax Due side
   Transfer total of 'Payments' VAT column to Tax Deductible side

Example illustrating the method of writing up the General Cash Book and balancing it at the end of the month

Assume that on 1 September the General Cash Book has a balance in hand of £1,500 During the month the following transactions take place:

Receipts		Ref.		Payments		Ref.	
			£				£
Sep 25	Credit sales (payments from customers)	CJ1	246.00	Sep 1	Petty cash	PCB1	50.00
				15	Credit purchases (payments to suppliers)	PJ1	501.49
27	Cash sales	NL/C1	57.50 (VAT 7.50)	17	Wages	WB1	105.32
29	Sale of machine	NL/MZ	97.75 (VAT 12.75)	20	Purchase of machine	NL/M2	115.00 (VAT 15.00)
				30	Petty cash	PCB1	19.27

The above transaction would appear in the Cash Book as shown in Example 28.

Calculation of Closing Balance

Opening balance + Receipts total – Payments total = Closing balance
£1,500.00 + £401.25 – £1,136.08 = £765.17

Updating of VAT Summary

See Example 29.

	RECEIPTS							PAYMENTS								
① DATE	② DETAILS	③ FOL.	④ SALES LEDGER	⑤ OTHER RECEIPTS	⑥ BALANCE	⑦ VAT	⑧ DATE	⑨ DETAILS	⑩ FOL.	⑪ PURCHASES LEDGER	⑫ PETTY CASH	⑬ WAGES	⑭ OTHER PAYMENTS	⑮ BALANCE	⑯ VAT
Sept 1	BROUGHT FWD				1500 00			BROUGHT FWD							
25	Credit Sales	CJ1	246 00				Sept 1	Petty Cash	PCB1		50 00				
27	Cash Sales	NL/C1		57 50		7 50	15	Credit Purchases	PJ1	501 49					
29	Sale of Machine	NL/M2		97 75		12 75	17	Wages	WB1			105 32			
							20	Purchase of Machine	NL/M2				115 00		15 00
							30	Petty Cash	PCB1		19 27				
							30	Balance	c/d					1110 17	
			246 00	155 25	1500 00	20 25				501 49	69 27	105 32	115 00	1110 17	15 00

Example 28

VAT Summary		Period from 1 September to 30 November				Bold Figures refer to appropriate Boxes on Quarterly VAT Return (VAT 100)			
Tax Due				**Outputs**	**Tax Deductible**				**Inputs**
Date	Ref.	Details	Output Tax	Output Values (Sales etc.)	Date	Ref.	Details	Input Tax	Input Values (Purchases etc.)
		Brought Forward							
Sept 30	CB1	Cash Book	20 25	135 00	Sept 30	CB1	Cash Book	60 00	400 00

Example 29

How to balance the cash book

Procedure

Step 1   Add analysis columns on 'Receipts' side of Cash Book as follows:

Column 4 + Column 5 + Column 6
£246.00 + £155.25 + £1,500.00 = £1,901.25

Do *not* enter these totals in the Cash Book at this stage and do *not* include VAT column total.

Step 2   Add analysis columns on 'Payments' side of Cash Book as follows:

Column 11 + Column 12 + Column 13 + Column 14 + Column 15
£501.49 + £69.27 + £105.32 + £115.00 + Nil = £791.08

Do *not* enter these totals in the Cash Book at this stage and do *not* include VAT column total.

Step 3   To calculate 'Balance' at the end of period deduct smaller total from the larger total as shown in Steps 1 and 2

Total calculated in Step 1 less Total calculated in Step 2 = Balance
£1,901.25 – £791.08 = £1,110.17

Step 4   If total in Step 1 is greater than total in Step 2 this balance is *entered* at (1) (see Example 30) on 'Payments' side as £1,110.17.

If total in Step 2 is greater than Step 1 this balance is *entered* at (2) on 'Receipts' side.

Step 5   After entering the balance add all columns including VAT on 'Receipts' and 'Payments' sides of Cash Book and *enter* the totals as shown at (3).

Step 6   If closing balance is recorded on 'Payments' side of Cash Book then the opening balance is entered on 'Receipts' side of Cash Book and the date and narrative 'Balance' 'b/d' is shown opposite the amount at (4).

If closing balance is recorded on 'Receipts' side of Cash Book then the opening balance is entered on 'Payments' side of Cash Book and the date and narrative 'Balance' 'b/d' is shown opposite the amount at (5).

Step 7   Proving the totals:

Columns 4 + 5 + 6 = Columns 11 + 12 + 13 + 14 + 15
£246.00 + £155.25 + £1,500.00
= £501.49 + £69.27 + £105.32 + £115.00 + £1,110.17
£1,901.25 = £1,901.25

The VAT columns are excluded from this calculation.

CBI	RECEIPTS						PAYMENTS								
①	②	③	④	⑤	⑥	⑦	⑧	⑨	⑩	⑪	⑫	⑬	⑭	⑮	⑯
DATE	DETAILS	FOL.	SALES LEDGER	OTHER RECEIPTS	BALANCE	VAT	DATE	DETAILS	FOL.	¹ PURCHASES LEDGER	² PETTY CASH	³ WAGES	⁴ OTHER PAYMENTS	⁵ BALANCE	⁶ VAT
Sept 1	BROUGHT FWD				1500 00			BROUGHT FWD							
25	Credit Sales	CJ1	246 00				Sept 1	Petty Cash	PCB1		50 00				
27	Cash Sales	NL/C1		57 50		7 50	15	Credit Purchases	PJ1	501 49					
29	Sale of Machine	NL/M2		97 75		12 75	17	Wages	WB1			105 32			
							20	Purchase of Machine	NL/M2				115 00		15 00
						Enter amount here	30	Petty Cash	PCB1		19 27				
					② ← here		30	Balance	c/d					③ 1110 17	
			246 00	155 25	1500 00	20 25 ←		③ →		501 49	69 27	105 32	115 00	1110 17	15 00
Oct 1	Balance	b/d		④ 1110 17										⑤ ← Enter amount here	

Example 30

195

How to keep a running balance in the general cash book (if necessary)

1 On the receipts side

Previous amount in Column 6 + Receipt = New amount in Column 6, e.g.

£1,500 + £246 = £1,746

2 On the payments side

Previous amount in Column 15 + Payment = New amount in Column 15, e.g.

Nil + £50 = £50

How to calculate the balance on the cash book

Under this method, the balance is the difference between the running totals on each side (see Example 31), i.e.

Balance = Last figure in Column 6 – Last figure in Column 15

where last amount in Column 6 is the larger, or

Balance = Last figure in Column 15 – Last figure in Column 6

where last amount in Column 15 is the larger.

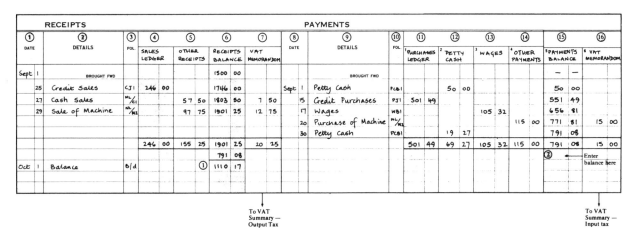

RECEIPTS							PAYMENTS									
①	②	③	④	⑤	⑥	⑦	⑧	⑨	⑩	⑪	⑫	⑬	⑭	⑮	⑯
DATE	DETAILS	FOL.	SALES LEDGER	OTHER RECEIPTS	RECEIPTS BALANCE	VAT MEMORANDUM	DATE	DETAILS	FOL.	¹ PURCHASES LEDGER	² PETTY CASH	³ WAGES	⁴ OTHER PAYMENTS	⁵ PAYMENTS BALANCE	⁶ VAT MEMORANDUM
Sept 1	BROUGHT FWD				1500 00			BROUGHT FWD						— —	
25	Credit Sales	CJ1	246 00		1746 00		Sept 1	Petty Cash	PCB1		50 00			50 00	
27	Cash Sales	ML/C1		57 50	1803 50	7 50	15	Credit Purchases	PJ1	501 49				551 49	
29	Sale of Machine	NL/N2		97 75	1901 25	12 75	17	Wages	WB1			105 32		656 81	
							20	Purchase of Machine	ML/N2				115 00	771 81	15 00
							30	Petty Cash	PCB1		19 27			791 08	
			246 00	155 25	1901 25	20 25				501 49	69 27	105 32	115 00	791 08	15 00
					791 08									② ← Enter balance here	
Oct 1	Balance	b/d		①	1110 17										

To VAT Summary — Output Tax

To VAT Summary — Input tax

Example 31

How to record end of period balance

To record end of period balance deduct the last amount shown in Column 15 from the last amount in Column 6 thus:

Column 6 – Column 15 = Balance
£1,901.25 – £791.08 = £1,110.17

This balance is entered at 1 on 'Receipts' side. If the last amount in Column 15 is greater than the last amount in Column 6 then the balance is entered at 2 on 'Payments' side.

Recording entries in the petty cash book

Procedure

Step 1   Complete a Petty Cash Voucher showing full details of the payment and have it countersigned by person to whom the money is paid.

Step 2   Head up analysis columns on 'Cash Paid' side as appropriate, e.g. Travelling Expenses, Postages, etc.

Step 3   Enter opening balance on 'Cash Received' side of Petty Cash Book *or* enter 'Imprest' amount from General Cash Book.

Step 4   Record payments on 'Cash Paid' side as follows:

Enter the total amount of each payment in 'Amount' column
Enter the VAT on each expense payment in the VAT column
Enter the amount of the payment ex VAT in the appropriate analysis column

Step 5   Balance the Petty Cash Book as explained in next section.

Step 6   Update VAT Summary:

Enter the total of the VAT column of the Petty Cash Book in the Tax Deductible side of the VAT Summary
Enter the value of payments made which is the 'Amount' column total less the VAT column total in the Petty Cash Book.

Step 7   File the Petty Cash Vouchers in order of entry in the Petty Cash Book.

Example

A. Smith has the following transactions involving the Petty Cash Book:

1 September	Received 'Imprest' amount from General Cash Book £50.00
2 September	Paid travelling expenses £5.25
9 September	Paid postage £3.10
15 September	Paid stationery £10.92 (VAT £1.42)
30 September	Amount transferred from General Cash Book to make up cash balance to 'Imprest' amount.

Step 1   Complete Petty Cash Voucher for payment.

Step 2   Head up analysis columns.

Step 3   Enter balance or 'Imprest' amount on Cash Received side.

Step 4   Enter payments.

Step 5   Balance Petty Cash Book (see Example 32).

Step 6   Update VAT Summary (see Example 33).

Step 7   File Petty Cash Vouchers in order of entry in Petty Cash Book.

PCB1															
Cash Received			**Cash Paid**									**Petty Cash Book**			
Date	Folio	Amount		Date	Details	Voucher Number	Amount		1 VAT		2 TRAVEL		3 POSTAGE	4 STATIONERY	
					Brought Forward										
Sept 1	CB1	50	00	Sept 2	Travelling Expenses	1	5	25			5	25			
30	CB1	19	27	9	Postages	2	3	10					3	10	
				15	Stationary	3	10	92	1	42					9 50
							19	27	1	42	5	25	3	10	9 50
				30	Balance	c/d	50	00							
		£69	27				£69	27							
Oct 1	b/d	50	00												

Example 32

VAT Summary			Period from 1 September to 30 November						Bold Figures refer to appropriate Boxes on Quarterly VAT Return (VAT 100)			
Tax Due					Outputs	**Tax Deductible**					Inputs	
Date	Ref.	Details		Output Tax	Output Values (Sales etc.)	Date	Ref.	Details		Input Tax	Input Values (Purchases etc.)	
		Brought Forward										
						Sept 30	PCB1	Petty Cash		1 42	17	85

Example 33

How to balance the petty cash book

Procedure

Step 1 Total 'Amount' column on 'Cash Paid' side of the Petty Cash Book as indicated at (1) in Example 34.

Step 2 Enter total of 'Amount' column on 'Cash Paid' side as indicated at (2).

Step 3 Enter total shown at (2) in the 'Amount' column 'Cash Received' side of Petty Cash Book and enter date and General Cash Book folio opposite. This amount will be the sum to be transferred from the General Cash Book to the Petty Cash Book referred to as the 'Imprest' amount.

Step 4 Add analysis columns 1, 2, 3 and 4 and enter total at the foot of each column.

Step 5 Enter 'Imprest' amount at (5) in 'Amount' column on 'Cash Paid' side and show date and the narrative 'Balance' opposite.

Step 6 Add 'Amount' columns on 'Cash Received' and 'Cash Paid' sides of Petty Cash Book. These amounts should be equal and totalled on the same line.

Step 7 Enter 'Imprest' amount at (7) in 'Amount' column 'Cash received' side and show date opposite. This amount must be the same as shown at (5).

PCB1																
Cash Received			**Cash Paid**										**Petty Cash Book**			
Date	Folio	Amount		Date	Details		Voucher Number		Amount		1 VAT		2 TRAVEL	3 POSTAGE	4 STATIONERY
						Brought Forward									
Sept 1	CB1	50 00		Sept 2	Travelling Expenses		1		5 25				5 25		
30	CB1	③ 19 27		9	Postages		2	①	3 10					3 10	
				15	Stationary		3		10 92		1 42				
								②	19 27		1 42		5 25	3 10	9 50
				30	Balance		c/d	⑤	50 00						
		£ 69 27			⑥				£ 69 27			STEP 4			
Oct 1	b/d	⑦ 50 00													

Example 34

Completing the VAT summary sheet

Procedure

Step 1 Record the totals of the following documents in the VAT Summary Sheet:

Tax Due side (outputs)
Sales Day Book
Sales Returns Day Book (bracket totals)
Cash Book (Receipts side)

Tax Deductible side (inputs)
Purchases Day Book
Purchases Returns Day Book (bracket totals)
Cash Book (Payments side)
Petty Cash Book (Payments side)

Step 2 Add Output Tax column and enter total in Box 1; add Output Values column and enter total in Box 9. Add Input Tax column and enter total in Box 5; add Input Values column and enter total in Box 10. In each case subtract figures in brackets.

Step 3 Complete Boxes 2 and 3 and show total in Box 4. Complete Box 6 and show total in Box 7.

Step 4 Deduct Box 7 from Box 4 and enter difference in Box 8 (Tax Due) or Box 8 (Tax Deductible).

Step 5 Transfer information to VAT 100 Form.

Example

Record the following information (summarised from previous examples) in the VAT Summary Sheet:

		Ref.	Tax £	Values £
12 September	Purchases Day Book	PDB1	25.60	255.95
18 September	Sales Day Book	SDB1	42.29	523.28
19 September	Purchases Returns Day Book	PRDB1	4.78	31.90
29 September	Sales Returns Day Book	SRDB1	3.64	24.30
30 September	Cash Book (Receipts side)	CB1	20.25	135.00
30 September	Cash Book (Payments side)	CB1	15.00	100.00
30 September	Petty Cash Book (Payments side)	PCB1	1.42	17.85

The recording should be as shown in Example 35.

202

VAT Summary									Bold Figures refer to appropriate Boxes on Quarterly VAT Return (VAT 100)	

Period from **1 September** to **30 November**

Tax Due				Outputs		Tax Deductible				Inputs	
Date	Ref.	Details	Output Tax	Output Values (Sales etc.)		Date	Ref.	Details	Input Tax	Input Values (Purchases etc.)	
		Brought Forward									
Sept 18	SDB1	Sales	42 | 29	523 | 28		Sept 12	PDB1	Credit Purchases	25 | 60	255 | 95	
Sept 29	SRDB1	Sales Returns	(3 | 64)	(24 | 30)		Sept 19	PRJB1	Purchases Returns	(4 | 78)	(31 | 90)	
Sept 30	CB1	Cash Book	20 | 25	135 | 00		Sept 30	PCB1	Petty Cash	1 | 42	17 | 85	
						Sept 30	CB1	Cash Book	15 | 00	100 | 00	

> NOTE: In practice details for the three months ending 30 November would be included in this summary

		Carried Forward									
Tax due in this period		**1**	58 | 90								
Add Tax due on Imported Goods and Goods from Bonded Warehouse etc.		**2**									
Underdeclarations in previous periods		**3**				Tax Deductible for this period	**5**	37 | 24			
						Overdeclarations in previous periods	**6**				
Total Tax Due for Period (1+2+3)		**4**	58 | 90			Total Tax Deductible for Period (5+6)	**7**	37 | 24			
Net Tax Repayable (if tax deductible exceeds tax due 7-4)		**8**				Net Tax Payable (if tax due exceeds tax deductible 4-7)	**8**	21 | 66			
Total Value of Outputs for Period (excluding tax)		**9**		633 | 98		Total Value of Inputs for Period (excluding tax)	**10**			341 | 90	

Example 35

In Conclusion: Your Business and the Microcomputer

At some time in the future you may decide to purchase a microcomputer to replace your manual system of bookkeeping. When this stage is reached the following points should be considered:

☐ The disciplines of a good manual system of bookkeeping are still essential to the successful operation of a computerised system.

☐ The introduction of a microcomputer system will not of itself resolve the bookkeeping problems in the business if the present system of recording is inefficiently operated.

☐ Before installing a microcomputer system ensure that your existing manual system of bookkeeping is operating efficiently and the information is accurate and up-to-date.

☐ To ensure a smooth changeover it is advisable to operate the manual and computerised system in tandem for a short period of time so that any operational difficulties encountered in the installation of the microcomputer will not delay the production of financial information to the business.

☐ It is essential that there is in operation a satisfactory system of recording basic information and input data for the computer before installation takes place. Balances on the ledger accounts must be accurate before being transferred to the microcomputer system. Time should be spent with the supplier of the equipment ensuring that the information is being collected in the business in a form suitable for recording on to the microcomputer.

As the purchase of a microcomputer and programs usually means a considerable investment for a small business, it is necessary to carefully examine the type of system most suited to the business to ensure that it will be capable of providing the necessary financial and other information required by management to enable them to conduct the business efficiently and effectively.

The following are some additional comments that you should carefully consider before purchasing a microcomputer system.

☐ Is the supplier of the microcomputer system an agent or do they manufacture the system? It is preferable that the supplier is the manufacturer of the equipment and also provides the software as well as being responsible for maintenance. In this instance you have only to negotiate with one party should any problems in the hardware and software arise. In other words you are looking for a 'total service' from your supplier.

☐ Does the supplier provide adequate facilities for staff training? It is essential that the supplier can provide on-site staff training and preferably also provide central or regional staff training facilities not only at the installation stage but as a continuing service.

☐ What are the repair and maintenance services provided by the supplier? This is a most important matter which has to be examined prior to purchase of the equipment since businesses using computers require the equipment to be operating continuously and cannot afford to have it out of action for long periods of time due to breakdowns. The maintenance contract should be studied in detail to ensure that the terms and conditions stated are capable of being carried out by the supplier to meet the demands of the user.

□ Are the programs being supplied with the microcomputer tailored to meet the requirements of the business? Care has to be exercised to make certain that the supplier does not provide programs which do not meet the specific requirements of the business and that you are not persuaded to change your system to suit the supplier's program. Remember that the programs supplied must satisfy the needs of the business if the information provided by them is to be of value.

□ Does the supplier provide a comprehensive instruction manual? This is a necessary document required by the business so that clear and easy-to-follow instructions are given to the operating staff covering all aspects of the equipment and its various applications.

YOU'VE GOT THE BOOK. NOW GET THE SYSTEM.

The Kalamazoo book~keeping system for small businesses

The accounting methods described in the following section also serve as step-by-step instructions for Set-up — the Kalamazoo book-keeping system for small businesses.

If you're starting up in business, (even if you've been going for some time), Set-up has been designed for you. Within one simple system, you can take care of all your basic accounting needs. Sales accounts, purchases accounts, cash book, petty cash book, and VAT.

In a simplified form, Set-up is based on many of the techniques and ideas which have made Kalamazoo a household name in business systems.

(Our range is currently used by over 125,000 firms in Britain alone, so you'll be in good company).

Quite simply, Kalamazoo Set-up gives you the means to keep your books up-to-date, accurately and efficiently, with no messing.

And it gives you the management information you need to keep you firmly in control of your business, right from the start.

Now doesn't that sound like a good idea?

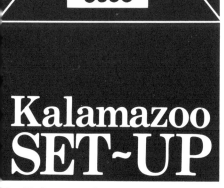

Kalamazoo SET~UP

The Kalamazoo book~keeping system for small businesses

Kalamazoo
business systems